Inside Poetry Out

Inside Poetry Out

An Introduction to Poetry

John O. Hayden

Nelson-Hall *nh* Chicago

"Icy Harvest" from *A Sense of Place* by Celeste Turner Wright: copyright 1973 by Celeste Turner Wright; "Death in Leamington" from *Collected Poems* by John Betjeman: copyright 1932 by John Murray, Ltd., and Houghton Mifflin Co.; "Grandparents" from *Life Studies* by Robert Lowell: reprinted by permission of Farrar, Straus & Giroux, Inc., copyright © 1956, 1959 by Robert Lowell; "Apparently with no Surprise" by Emily Dickinson reprinted by permission of the publishers and the Trustees of Amherst College from *The Poems of Emily Dickinson*, edited by Thomas H. Johnson, Cambridge, Mass.: The Belknap Press of Harvard University Press, copyright 1951, © 1955, 1979 by the President and Fellows of Harvard College; "The Villain" by W. H. Davies: copyright 1963 by Jonathan Cape, Ltd., reprinted from *The Complete Poems of W. H. Davies* by permission of Wesleyan University Press; "The Aliens" by W. H. Auden reprinted by permission of Curtis Brown Ltd.: the poem originally appeared in *The New Yorker*, copyright 1970 by W. H. Auden; Excerpt from "Autumn Chapter in a Novel" from *Thom Gunn: Selected Poems* by Thom Gunn: copyright © 1979 by Thom Gunn, reprinted by permission of Farrar, Straus & Giroux, Inc. and Faber and Faber, Ltd.; "The Bottom Line" by Mary Dougherty, copyright Mary Dougherty, 1982; "Love's Noon" and "Song" by John Ellsworth, copyright John Ellsworth, 1982; "Gang Rape" and "For the Blue-Eyed Smiler on the Bus" by Steve Ellzey, copyright Steve Ellzey, 1982; "Basey's Bike" by Ken Jones, copyright James Kenneth Jones, 1982; "Spider Killing" by Hans Ostrom, copyright Hans Ostrom, 1978; "Calm and Fear" by Hans Ostrom, copyright Hans Ostrom, 1982.

Copyright © 1983 by John O. Hayden

Manufactured in the United States of America

10 9 8 7 6 5 4 3 2 1

The paper in this book is pH neutral (acid-free).

Contents

Preface

This book is designed to introduce students to the serious study of poetry. I would not, however, hesitate to propose its usefulness to anyone who would like either to learn about poetry or to refresh his mind about it without getting involved with more specialized and advanced studies.

It has been my experience that the best way to learn to understand poetry is to analyze one poem after another. The sequence of chapters in fact has been organized to get the students interested in poetry as quickly as possible. To this end I have tried to present them early with information and terminology that will allow them personally to analyze poems.

No doubt the most original aspect of the book is the organization of the material. Instead of continually introducing different poems or parts of poems in discussing various points about poetry, I present five poems at the

beginning of the text and bring as much subsequent discussion as possible to bear upon these poems. For example, I discuss the meaning of the five poems in chapter 2,
use examples from them to discuss versification in chapter 3, and so on. Not only does this procedure cut down
on unnecessary quotations and confusion, but it should
be of considerable value by the end of the text. For, since
the model explications are written about these five poems
as well, the student can see the possibilities of explication and how it is arrived at. Rather than suffering from
the usual awe engendered by reading an explication of an
unfamiliar poem (How did he see all those things?!), the
student will have followed the discussion of the poems
throughout the previous text and will *understand* where
it all came from.

For those who have no need to write about poetry, the
explications at the end (Appendix I) will serve in any case
to make the book a self-contained unit. After having followed discussions of the same five poems through the
book, the reader will then have available in the formal
explications organized readings of each poem. There is
thus a wholeness and unity not often found in such a
text.

The poems included in Appendix II, "Some Additional
Poems Suitable for Analysis," are intended to supply the
reader with material on which to apply newly developed
analytical skills. The poems in question are little known,
and while not necessarily great or flawless, they are, I
believe, interesting and successful poems, and more im-
portantly, they are well supplied with poetic devices as
well as impressive meter or imagery.

The last chapter provides students with guidance on
writing an explication of a poem. The attempt at a kind
of standardization, also demonstrated in the model expli-

cations, is not intended to stifle more individual approaches but should suggest some possibilities.

As for the content of the other chapters, the discussions are as closely tied to traditional and contemporary theory as I could make them. There is no reason, so far as I know, to treat literary matters from scratch, as if no one had ever dealt with them before. Disagreements with the theories as I've set them forth can in any case be easily accommodated. As I hope will be clear, I'm aware disagreement by some theorists already exists; it would be astounding were it otherwise, considering the interest and involvement in things literary. I hope disagreements of students and instructors with the text (and with each other) will lead to illuminating discussions. The presence of traditional and standard views should not hamper the process; on the contrary, without some center to turn to (and from) it seems to me that disagreement and illumination are more, rather than less, difficult to attain.

Dover Beach

The sea is calm tonight,
The tide is full, the moon lies fair
Upon the straits;—on the French coast the light
Gleams and is gone; the cliffs of England stand,
Glimmering and vast, out in the tranquil bay.   5
Come to the window, sweet is the night-air!
Only, from the long line of spray
Where the sea meets the moon-blanched land,
Listen! you hear the grating roar
Of pebbles which the waves draw back, and fling,   10
At their return, up the high strand,
Begin, and cease, and then again begin,
With tremulous cadence slow, and bring
The eternal note of sadness in.

Sophocles long ago   15
Heard it on the Aegean, and it brought
Into his mind the turbid ebb and flow
Of human misery; we
Find also in the sound a thought,
Hearing it by this distant northern sea.   20

The Sea of Faith
Was once, too, at the full, and round earth's shore
Lay like the folds of a bright girdle furled.
But now I only hear
Its melancholy, long, withdrawing roar,   25
Retreating, to the breath
Of the night-wind, down the vast edges drear
And naked shingles of the world.

Ah, love, let us be true
To one another! for the world, which seems   30
To lie before us like a land of dreams,
So various, so beautiful, so new,
Hath really neither joy, nor love, nor light,
Nor certitude, nor peace, nor help for pain;
And we are here as on a darkling plain   35
Swept with confused alarms of struggle and flight,
Where ignorant armies clash by night.

Matthew Arnold (1822–1888)

Grandparents

They're altogether otherworldly now,
those adults champing for their ritual Friday spin
to pharmacist and five-and-ten in Brockton.
Back in my throw-away and shaggy span
of adolescence, Grandpa still waves his stick   5
like a policeman;
Grandmother, like a Mohammedan, still wears her thick
lavender mourning and touring veil;
the Pierce Arrow clears its throat in a horse-stall.
Then the dry road dust rises to whiten   10
the fatigued elm leaves—
the nineteenth century, tired of children, is gone.
They're all gone into a world of light; the farm's my own.

The farm's my own!
Back there alone   15
I keep indoors, and spoil another season.
I hear the rattley little country gramophone
racking its five foot horn:
"O Summer Time!"
Even at noon here the formidable   20
Ancien Regime still keeps nature at a distance. Five
green shaded light bulbs spider the billiards-table;
no field is greener than its cloth,
where Grandpa, dipping sugar for us both,
once spilled his demitasse.   25
His favorite ball, the number three,
still hides the coffee stain.

Never again
to walk there, chalk our cues,

insist on shooting for us both.   30
Grandpa! Have me, hold me, cherish me!
Tears smut my fingers. There
half my life-lease later,
I hold an *Illustrated London News*—;
disloyal still,   35
I doodle handlebar
mustaches on the last Russian Czar.

                              Robert Lowell (1917–1977)

Death in Leamington

She died in the upstairs bedroom
By the light of the ev'ning star
That shone through the plate glass window
From over Leamington Spa.

Beside her the lonely crochet   5
Lay patiently and unstirred,
But the fingers that would have work'd it
Were dead as the spoken word.

And Nurse came in with the tea-things
Breast high 'mid the stands and chairs—   10
But Nurse was alone with her own little soul,
And the things were alone with theirs.

She bolted the big round window,
She let the blinds unroll,
She set a match to the mantle,   15
She covered the fire with coal.

And 'Tea!' she said in a tiny voice
'Wake up! It's nearly five.'
Oh! Chintzy, chintzy cheeriness,
Half dead and half alive!   20

Do you know that the stucco is peeling?
Do you know that the heart will stop?
From those yellow Italianate arches
Do you hear the plaster drop?

Nurse looked at the silent bedstead,   25
At the gray, decaying face,
As the calm of a Leamington ev'ning
Drifted into the place.

She moved the table of bottles
Away from the bed to the wall,   30
And tiptoeing gently over the stairs
Turned down the gas in the hall.

John Betjeman (1906–   )

when faces called flowers

when faces called flowers float out of the ground
and breathing is wishing and wishing is having—
but keeping is downward and doubting and never
—it's april(yes, april;my darling)it's spring!
yes the pretty birds frolic as spry as can fly   5
yes the little fish gambol as glad as can be
(yes the mountains are dancing together)

when every leaf opens without any sound
and wishing is having and having is giving—
but keeping is doting and nothing and nonsense   10
—alive;we're alive,dear:it's(kiss me now)spring!
now the pretty birds hover so she and so he
now the little fish quiver so you and so i
(now the mountains are dancing,the mountains)

when more than was lost has been found has been found   15
and having is giving and giving is living—
but keeping is darkness and winter and cringing
—it's spring(all our night becomes day)o,it's spring!
all the pretty birds dive to the heart of the sky
all the little fish climb through the mind of the sea   20
(all the mountains are dancing;are dancing)

e. e. cummings (1894–1962)

Icy Harvest

To fill the storehouse on the bank a crew
Were sawing channels in the frozen lake
And pushing heavy blocks that bobbed along;
The ice-crop, mealed with sawdust, garnered up,
Would freshen summer at the great hotel.   5
Old Amos gave the child a pointed pole
And let her work an hour at his side;
The sunshine twinkled on the floating ice.
   But later, when she skimmed away on skates
To see the woodsmen hauling logs across,   10
She found them clustered where a team had drowned:
Two giant horses, plunging through the ice,
Strapped to their loaded sledge, had buffeted
Until their hearts had reached a stony stop.
The bodies, sodden from the water, lay   15
Enormous on the ice-road, glazing stiff,
With desperation frozen in their eyes.
Thick tongues protruded; icicles encroached
On mouths that often, warm and velvety,
Had lipped the sugar from her proffered palm.   20
   Delight was murdered, for the glassy miles
Revealed this other possibility;
Terror now gaped where she had moved secure
In the deceitful glitter of the sun.

Celeste Turner Wright (1906–   )

1

The Nature of Poetry
(and how to read it)

Many definitions of poetry have been attempted. Almost every textbook on poetry contains at least one; the challenge of capturing in words something so elusive is apparently very strong. But no single definition has been found satisfactory either to old hands or to newcomers, and perhaps it is better to approach the nature of poetry from a larger view rather than to narrow it down to a brief definition.

Today there is not even a general agreement about the universal appeal of poetry. Until perhaps two hundred years ago, before the great expansion of printing techniques and literacy, most of those who could read at all would have read poetry for enjoyment and would likely have talked about their reading as well. Then, with the expansion of the reading public in the nineteenth century and the fracturing of that public into lowbrow, middlebrow, and highbrow, poetry became largely a highbrow concern, until today few people outside universities and metropolitan coteries deal with any poetry except in greeting cards and popular songs. But the situation was not always so, and consequently it is not necessary to see the reading of poetry as an elitist occupation.

Poetry does, however, seem important to a fairly large group of people, and this fact should lead the casual observer to ask why the appeal exists. What is poetry that it should attract seemingly intelligent people away from other sorts of entertainment, even from serious prose fiction and drama? What am I missing? Everyone knows at least a few people who don't really enjoy eating; although they have a clear advantage over others in controlling their weight, one doesn't have to be a gourmet to be convinced that they are missing one of the enjoyments of life. Is poetry like that too? Or is it a colossal fraud, a way of keeping the undereducated or the uninitiated in their place?

To provide answers it is unnecessary to resort to bald assertions about what poetry is and is not, as some of its proponents have done. For there is considerable theory recorded about the nature of literature, from Aristotle to the present. By calling upon this great body of thought, perhaps we can arrive at some general notion of what poetry is and does.

Probably one of the most important elements of literature is its relationship to life; at least that is the side of literature to which theorists first turned their attention. While some minor theorists in the nineteenth century saw literature as *merely* an expression of the writer's feelings, the traditional view from Aristotle to the present has been to see literature as mimetic—that is, as representing life or human experience either directly or implicitly. As a matter of fact, right from the beginning the enjoyment of literature has been said to derive to some extent from the recognition of the truth-to-life in a work of literature.

Truth-to-*fact*—to literal or historical fact—is not necessary in literature, however. Literature is not documentary; it need possess neither photographic realism nor reportorial accuracy. For Aristotle qualified his mimetic theory by pointing out the universal aspects of literature. Literature differs from history, he argued (in the *Poetics*, chapter 9), in that literature deals with the normal side of life, the general state of affairs, while history by its nature must stick to details, to the "facts."

The literary writer, of course, also uses details, but selects them to point up the norm in human behavior. There is even an implied balance in this traditional view: the writer who goes too far in the direction of mimesis falls into the trap of presenting the unusual, the topical, the odd, which do not interest for long; going too far in the direction of universality, on the other hand, results in the merely typical, the stereotyped, which also do not engage the interest of serious readers.

But is that all there is to literature—a selective representation of life that pleases for one reason or another? Has it no serious function that would repay a busy person who invested the time and energy to read and understand it? Aristotle's *Poetics* provides no such reason: he wrote little about any purpose of literature. Pleasure is mentioned, of course; it is almost always introduced by literary theorists, probably because it is so obviously involved. Discussion of moral issues and considerations also abounds in the *Poetics*, yet without any clear indication of their innate role or necessity in literature. We must turn to later members of the tradition for discussion of any purpose for literature beyond pleasure.

The next major theorist, Horace, provided a view of the moral purpose of literature that lasted for some eighteen centuries. In his *Ars Poetica* he set forth what came to be known as the Horatian formula—namely, that literature teaches and pleases. Horace established a standard way of seeing the teaching side of literature: it worked through the presentation of precepts or, more usually, of examples. One either supplied the reader with a direct moral statement a la Aesop's *Fables* or showed vice punished and virtue rewarded in a story, and the reader was consequently edified. Such a view should be called *moralistic* rather than *moral*; but, more important, it is disconnected from the view of mimesis/universality and thus has no real support from the nature of literature itself. It is prescriptive, not descriptive: it derives from what these theorists thought literature *ought* to do rather than what they saw that it actually *does*.

Then, by the early nineteenth century, a new way of seeing the teaching function of literature had emerged. Looking to literature itself, William Wordsworth in his famous preface to *Lyrical Ballads* (1800) agreed that literature had a moral function but argued that that function was indirect, *not* through precept nor example. The poet, Wordsworth claimed, wrote in such a way "that the understanding of the [reader] . . . must necessarily be in some degree enlightened, and his affections ameliorated." That is, poetry (and literature in general) makes one more aware of human experience and sharpens one's emotional responses, both of which are important functions and both certainly moral in some sense. Matthew Arnold in an essay (1879) on Wordsworth expanded on this theory, which has by now become a standard view of literature, when its moral function is considered at all.

Literature's selective representation of life, to sum up Arnold's view, has a built-in purpose. That is, mimesis/universality presents the reader with experience selected and interpreted (directly or by implication) by a writer. Readers thus learn about life from literature; they understand the human condition just that much better; and they thereby become more-aware moral agents, better prepared than otherwise to make the moral decisions we all must make every day of our lives. For, like it or not, we are all moral agents.

What I have been describing as a traditional view of literature is not offered as a defense of poetry, nor is it an attempt to convince you that you ought to read poetry; it is merely a description of what remains, I believe, the central view of literature. Poetry in any case will finally have to be its own defense. Yet by this time you should at least recognize the potential of poetry to go beyond simple entertainment. It pleases, of course—one wouldn't likely read it otherwise—but it does much more.

Many inexperienced readers might readily accept the proposition that fiction does what I have argued that literature traditionally is supposed to do. *Poetry*, however, may seem less than pleasurable and enlightening to one who reads it only occasionally. But poetry and prose fiction are not really all that different; they are certainly not entirely separate and distinct. At points, in fact, as in prose poems, the distinction breaks down altogether. Both poetry and fiction represent in a selective way; both please (at least some people); and both convey or create an awareness of human experience.

In other words, the ends of both kinds of literature are the same. It is the means, especially the use of language and rhythm, that differ. Poetry most often deals with more experience in smaller space; and it deals with life so concisely that it calls attention to itself, its language and techniques. Also, the precision involved in the conciseness is one reason why a person can read poetry again and again with pleasure, whereas prose is most often read only once.

The language of poetry, which will be dealt with in more detail in chapter 5, is language packed with meaning. Every word counts in a successful poem, and there are no unnecessary words. And because a poem, by its concise handling of experience, draws attention to itself, it tends to be rich in figures of speech, especially metaphors, and in other devices to be considered in later chapters. Such expressions of course occur in prose fiction as well—prose has an economy of its own—but prose fiction, by dint of its length if nothing else, does not and cannot ask attention of the reader sufficient to allow for the density of language and figures that poetry employs.

The characteristic of poetry most often thought to distinguish it from prose is meter, and yet meter, as we shall see in chapter 3, is really only a more controlled form of the rhythm that is found in both prose and poetry. It is true that metered poetry tends toward more regularity or at least toward more pronounced rhythms, but some prose has very clear rhythm and some poetry very little. In fact, although meter was useful in distinguishing poetry from prose fiction before the nineteenth century, it is not of much use now; it is the criterion most likely to lead to distinctions that will not hold up.

A poem, in any case, asks immediately for attention. It demands that you spend some time and thought if you wish to appreciate it fully. And intelligent reading and discussion of poetry require some knowledge of how it works, what to expect, and what terms to use in talking about it. To provide such knowledge is what this book is all about.

Occasionally, however, someone will demur and suggest that reading poetry is nothing like reading music, where some knowledge of musical symbols must be acquired to make any sense of it. After all, poetry is composed of words, and we can all read. Such people also complain that they have trouble understanding a good many poems but are all too likely to blame the poets for being obscure; the possibility that their own ignorance of poetry is at fault does not often occur to them. Poetry, however, is not obscure by nature—it is written for all literate people; but poetry also requires craft to write and skill to read. The following suggestions are intended to prepare you to read poems on a beginning basis. Later chapters will develop more advanced skills.

Read the poem through once, without stopping at every problem word or passage. Try to get the drift of the poem, what the poet is trying to convey. This meaning or theme may not be in the form of a statement but may involve, for example, a dramatization or a kind of parable. Remember that the poem was written by another human being trying to communicate something; the writer is trying to tell you something about life, about human experience. Because of the conciseness and subtlety of poetry, the intended meaning may not be easy to see at first, but it is there, and finding it will become easier with practice.

At this point in your reading, look up in the dictionary any words you don't know or aren't sure of. A misreading of a poem or part of a poem can often turn on one word.

Read through the poem again, and see if your original idea of the poet's apparent intention works. If parts of the poem conflict with that idea, try to adapt it so that your reading takes them into account.

Read the poem a third time, this time aloud, and listen to the sound. A good deal of the pleasure and some of the meaning will come from the poet's treatment of sound, including both words and rhythm.

But remember: reading poetry is not meant to be a chore, even though it does require some effort on your part. The analysis of poetry which you have begun to learn will yield more understanding of the poems you read and consequently more pleasure. The counterview that the less we know about a poem the better, that we "murder to dissect," depends on a view of poetry as anything but an art. Any poem that does not survive analysis was not murdered by it—it was dead to start with.

2

Content
(meaning, genre, ideas)

$\mathbf{M}$odern theorists have questioned whether content and form can exist separately in literature. But as in any other discipline distinctions must be made in order to deal with the subject at all. Some aspects of poetry, such as meaning and ideas, are certainly more involved with the content of poems and can be discussed separately from their forms.

MEANING

The question of the meaning of a poem is obviously very important. What does the poem mean? is in fact usually the first question we ask. Until we arrive at an answer, we really cannot begin to answer (or even ask) further questions about the poetic techniques or their function.

Before rushing headlong into a discussion of meaning, however, we must confront a problem with the term *meaning* itself. The term implies a simple "solution" to the poem; to some extent it even suggests that there is a statement somewhere in the poem, a mini-paraphrase, either on or just below the surface. But poetic communication is not as easy as that. In a sense the meaning of a poem is the poem itself in all its complexity. And yet, while this view and others like it are useful as a warning, such theoretical principles do not take us very far; we must still deal with the poem.

Other ways of discussing meaning are to talk about the *theme* or the *subject* of the poem, to describe "what the poem is about." Or we can approach the meaning through the apparent intention of the poet: Why (apparently) did he write the poem? What was he trying to communicate? Although this latter approach is directed backwards to the origins of the poem, it actually asks the same question as is raised in a more direct approach: What does this poem convey? But the "indirect" approach has at least one advantage: by attempting to see the poem's reason for existence from the poet's point of view we tend to get away from the all-too-human tendency to make the poem convey what we as individuals want it to convey; and once we are fairly certain of the poet's intention, moreover, his strategy in working out that intention can provide a center from which to discuss the poem. As long as we follow such a procedure and are careful, we can, I believe, use any of the terms mentioned, including *meaning,* without raising insurmountable problems.

But we are assuming that we can discuss meaning in the singular. Perhaps, as beginning students sometimes insist, a poem's meaning is what each as an individual understands it to mean. Each reader thus would have a unique poem. According to this view, the intention of the poet, apparent or otherwise, finally doesn't matter. What matters is what we, the individual readers, get from the poem. On the other hand, some might argue—and a few students usually do—that there is only *one* meaning for a poem: it is what the poem means!

The fact that a poem often receives a large number of varied readings would seem to support the argument of the first group, although it doesn't demolish logically the position of the second, inasmuch as there could be an infinite number of different readings but only one that is correct. Practical considerations are what finally undermine the second view that there is only one valid reading. A few poems may be so simple and straightforward that everyone agrees on precisely what they mean, but for most poems (while there may be One True Reading for them existing in the mind of God) there is no way we can know the meaning for sure. There are simply too many variables in most poems; they are just too complex for a mere mortal to claim that *this* is what the poem *must* mean, and no other meaning is possible.

If, then, the one-true-meaning school is finally unacceptable, are we stuck with the every-man-for-himself view? No, luckily we're not. If we were, no intelligent discussion of poetry would be possible; we would all be exchanging idiosyncratic readings based on purely personal associations.

Luckily we have the text of the poem to turn to; it consists of words that have public meanings. That being the case, it is possible at least to conceive of a reading that is positively and inescapably mistaken. Every teacher has received at least one explication of a poem that is based on an ingenious twisting of meaning ripped out of context.

For example, we have the opening of the well-known poem, "Trees," by Joyce Kilmer:

> I think that I shall never see
> A poem lovely as a tree.

Here is a poem that surely qualifies as having an obvious, single meaning. A clever "over-reader," nevertheless, might start by pointing out that "I think" is a clear reference to the statement at the base of Descartes's metaphysics, "I think; therefore I am." Connected through rime, furthermore, are the words *see* and *tree*, too much of a coincidence to be anything other than the introduction into the poem of Bishop Berkeley's metaphysical question whether the *tree* falls in a forest when no one is there to *see* it. And thus we have the beginnings of a "philosophical" reading of the poem. Such wrongheaded readings, which build up a kind of inner logic of their own, are very difficult to dispute, although when you show how the meanings of the words have been wrenched out of context and associations have been established with no evidence, the errant explicator usually surrenders to reason.

On a less-uncertain level, readings may fail to take into account changes in word meanings, and such readings must be incorrect, unless one is willing to argue that poems are altogether bundles of words and devices that the reader can do with as he will, with meaning at the mercy not only of the individual but of time as well. William Wordsworth's "The Female Vagrant" (1798), for example, contains a number of words whose meanings have subsequently altered; at the time the poem was written, *strain* meant "to clasp tightly," *devoted* meant "doomed," and *amazed* meant "bewildered." To argue that knowledge of only the present meanings of these words would not lead to misreadings would be difficult, to say the least. Few are so reckless as to plunge into the consequent chaos; most will readily admit the possibility of a wrong reading. Once this crucial concession is made, the discussion can then move to a question of extent of misreading. *One* reading has some mistakes, but fewer than *this* one, which is less convincing than a *third*.

In fact, what each individual and all readers put together are after is *the most-likely reading,* and such an endeavor lends itself to rational discussion. We have a poetic context to turn to; we don't have to rely merely on our feelings (although feelings about poems can often be very helpful, especially when those feelings are trained). Your reading, someone might argue, relies on a misunderstanding of this phrase; or you missed the point of the metaphor; or the tone here is inconsistent with your version of this passage—all are valid arguments in discussing poetry.

Not every discussion about poetic meaning will arrive at agreement on the most-likely reading. Occasionally, two readings have equal forcefulness, and once that becomes evident, it is pointless to pursue the matter. But usually one reading will have more support from the context and present fewer problems than another. The sign of an intelligent approach to poetic meaning in any case is rational argument based on the poetic text.

Fairly recently a member of the Neo-Aristotelian school argued in favor of pursuing the apparent intention of the author of a literary work. But in fact no such admonition is necessary, for to attempt to discover the poet's apparent intention is a very natural way to read a poem and, as I've already insisted, is really no different from trying to establish what it is that the poem conveys. That word *apparent* (in apparent intention) is crucial, however, for without it we quickly get involved in biographical investigations. What did the poet *claim* was the meaning of his poem? He is surely the final authority.

Or is he? In 1946, W. K. Wimsatt, Jr., and Monroe Beardsley published a well-known article, "The Intentional Fallacy," which argues that what we have in the poem is not the poet's intention but his achievement and that the two need not be the same. In a very real way, once a poem is written it exists in its own right; the words and devices of which the poem consists are public and convey meaning. Such a position can probably be pushed too far, but it contains fewer problems than the alternative, popular in some circles today, that equates the poet's stated intention with the meaning of the poem. The stated intention can of course provide valuable information for understanding a poem; it's just that it's unreliable as the final word. And usually we don't have a statement from the poet anyway.

Genre

On a more practical level, it is often helpful to establish the apparent intention of poets by determining the *kind* of poem they seem to have written. *Genre,* the anglicized French term for "kind," denotes a well-established grouping of poems with certain ends in common, and often with shared conventions as well. Examples of genres would be epic, satirical, and pastoral. To establish the genre of a poem could obviously be of considerable help in determining its meaning. At an introductory level, most of the poems dealt with are short, and so only a few genres are actually encountered. What follows is intended not as a full-fledged discussion of genres, but only as a collection of practical points to be used in dealing with short poems.

Probably the easiest kind of poem to distinguish is *narrative.* Does the poem tell a story? Is there a "plot"? Of the five poems presented in the beginning of this book, "Icy Harvest" by Celeste Wright fits this description; it contains a narrative of an event in the life of a small girl. She begins by helping with the gathering of ice and then encounters a gruesome accident that has befallen two horses she knew as friends. Usually, short narratives do not exist for the mere sake of the story but involve some point the poet wishes to make. Here we are told almost directly that the child learns from the experience at the center of the story that there is an ugly side to nature as well as a beautiful one. The point is so clearly a major part of the motive behind the poem that it is not difficult to identify the poem as *narrative-reflective*. Few short poems in fact are strictly narrative.

Another kind of poem related to narrative is the *dramatic* poem, which presents a scene and a speaker or speakers. It does not simply tell a story, in other words, but rather dramatizes it. Such would be "Dover Beach" by Matthew Arnold. Here we have a speaker addressing his love about the desperate plight of civilization as he sees it and suggesting that a solution exists in their relationship. Again the kind of poem involved is not clearcut, for the reflections of the speaker about the world are surely at the center of the poem, leaving us the designation *dramatic-reflective* in this instance.

Reflective poems can also exist in their own right, providing an idea or situation along with some reflections. Robert Lowell's "Grandparents" offers an example: without story or dramatization, we are presented with the relationship between the speaker and his grandfather and some reflections on it.

Satire, another genre sometimes encountered among shorter poems, is most often defined as the ridicule of vice or folly for purposes of amendment. Sometimes satires are vicious (*Juvenalian*), but often they are lighter and more sympathetic (*Horatian*). Of the latter class is John Betjeman's "Death in Leamington," which describes the reaction of a nurse to the death of an old woman, her patient. The satire of this nurse (and probably of most nurses) is uncompromising but not bitter. She is shown to be mechanical, unfeeling, and therefore phony in her "friendly" relations with the old woman. There is possibly also a tacit reflection that it is easy for those caring for the sick to protect themselves after a while from the stress of witnessing pain by withdrawing sympathy altogether; but the main point of the poem is satiric.

A genre short by nature and most often unalloyed by reflection is the *lyric*. A bit more difficult to define, a lyric poem can be described as an expression by an individual (in the first person) of some strong emotion, such as love. "when faces called flowers" by e. e. cummings is a good example of a lyric; through his unusual dislocation of syntax and diction, he manages to give us a very original hymn to spring, one in which the speaker conveys the initial excitement of the season.

Short poems will fall under one or another of these categories, most often under a combination of two. What is important is to establish the apparent main intention of the poet. Once established, this information will take us a long way toward understanding the overall strategy (conscious or otherwise) of the poet in constructing the poem and finally toward analyzing how he used poetic devices to realize that strategy.

In analyzing Celeste Wright's "Icy Harvest," for example, once we have determined the genre as narrative-reflective, we can then move to the second step of examining the strategy by which the poet used the narrative elements to point up the reflective. The poem is given in three sections or verse paragraphs, and upon further scrutiny and thought, we can see that the strategy (or, if you prefer, logic) of the poem follows that structure as well. Since we have established the reflection given as the existence of an ugly side to life complementing the beautiful, it is not difficult to see that the first section sets the scene, the beautiful side of life; the second section brings us to the ugly reality; and the third clearly, but obliquely, sets out the consequent reflection. There is a good deal more to the strategy of the poem than that, of course; in fact, such an overview provides the means to deal with further details and techniques.

The strategy of Matthew Arnold's dramatic-reflective "Dover Beach" is only slightly more complex. The dramatic scene is set forth in the first section; the second acts as a transition between the sound of the ocean in the first and the metaphor of the "Sea of Faith" (or Christianity) in the third, with reflections on its gradual withdrawal and the drastic consequences in the last section. John Betjeman's satiric "Death in Leamington" is more straightforward in its strategy (if not in its tone); the only digression from a simple description of the death of the old woman and the movements of the nurse is the intrusion of the speaker in the fifth and sixth stanzas, in which he addresses the nurse and asks her to consider her attitudes. The lyric simplicity of the strategy of e. e. cummings's "when faces called flowers" is obscured by a very complicated repetition in stanza structure.

The strategy of Robert Lowell's reflective "Grandparents" is undoubtedly the most complicated among the five poems. Given the apparent intention of reflecting on the speaker's past relationship with his grandfather (and to a lesser extent with his grandmother), we can recognize the strategy of the first section in presenting the couple. After that, the strategy is more difficult to see, as the poet leads the attention of the reader around the farmhouse to more and more specific objects—the gramophone, the billiards table, the favorite ball ("the number three") and, finally the stain, which, by reminding the speaker of an event in his relationship with his grandfather, sets in motion the emotional outcry of the speaker. This outcry is followed by a brief description of the speaker's method of withdrawing from the emotion.

In each case the kind of poem involved allows one to see the strategy used, at least on a fairly wide view. More detailed working out of strategy and techniques will come in later chapters and in the full-length explications of the poems.

IDEAS

As late as the 1920s, poetry was taught mainly by reference to the lives of authors or to the times in which they lived. Poetry, that is, was treated more as document than as existing in its own right. Then a movement called the New Criticism (which is obviously not so new any more) came on the scene; its central precept was simply to turn to the text of the poem. To such New Critics as Cleanth Brooks, John Crowe Ransom, and I. A. Richards, we all owe a huge debt, for without their insistence on textual analysis, we might still be mainly involved with biography and literary history.

Unfortunately, the same movement that was responsible for our close scrutiny of texts and consequently deepened poetic appreciation was also responsible for severing connections between poetry and life. The contextualism that resulted left little room for questions about the realism of the characters or events or the validity or pertinence of the ideas of a poem. What became important instead was the inner consistency of a poem, how well the parts are integrated; I. A. Richards's theory of the "poetry of inclusion," for example, gave the highest ratings to poems that contained the most diverse elements with the least room for an ironic reading. Not all New Critics subscribed to this theory, but such was the thrust of the movement.

Partly because of this circumscription of the poem, there has been a tendency recently to undervalue or altogether ignore ideas in poems. But surely from the poet's point of view, if not the reader's, the ideas the poet is trying to convey are of central importance. Why otherwise would a writer bother to communicate at all? Only if you subscribe to contextual beliefs and see the "poem in itself" as an esthetic object in its own right can the ideas be overlooked. From a traditional standpoint, they certainly cannot be.

That the New Criticism should choose to overlook ideas in poetry as much as possible is not altogether surprising in view of the modern tendency toward critical relativism, for by focusing all attention onto the inside workings of the poem, questions of outside values need not arise. But such a stance is surely ironic considering the New Criticism's other emphasis, the organic unity of a poem. To refuse to take seriously the ideas of a poem with all their ramifications is surely to do havoc to its unity.

And besides, the ideas a poem contains are often among the most interesting things it has to offer. Matthew Arnold raises many questions in "Dover Beach": Is the modern condition as bad as the narrator seems to think? Does the absence of Christian values based on a Christian view of the world require us to find other foundations for the values we would like to retain? Is the narrator an escapist in his turning to his love for a way out of his dilemma? "Death in Leamington" by John Betjeman likewise raises the issue of the proper involvement of those who care for the sick and lonely. If the poet seems correct in the views projected, what does this say about the poem? And if incorrect?

To consider seriously the ideas in poetry, however, does not leave you home free. The question of one's attitude toward the particular ideas in a poem is, for example, a thorny one. Should the question of belief or disbelief have an effect on whether the reader values a poem, or even on whether one is capable at all of enjoying it? For example, a reader who is an atheist might find it difficult to appreciate *Paradise Lost* or any other religious poetry.

T. S. Eliot, in a published lecture on Keats and Shelley (1933), confronted the problem directly and proposed the principle that, as long as the reader feels that the ideas involved are intelligent and mature, there is no reason to feel put off by the poem in which they occur. For the purpose of enjoying the poem, the reader should accept the ideas in question as part of the machinery of the poem. One does not, according to this theory, have to be a medieval Catholic to appreciate Dante's *Divine Comedy* or a seventeenth-century Protestant to enjoy *Paradise Lost.*

But, Eliot continued, if a poet's ideas are such that a mature person would have trouble swallowing them, then the reader has a right to object and to criticize the poem accordingly. The example Eliot deals with is the poetry of Shelley, which occasionally proposes such ideas as the elimination of the institutions of marriage and government. You may of course disagree with these as instances of immature ideas, but unless you are willing to accept all ideas indiscriminately, you should consider the validity of Eliot's principle. Intellectual indifference is not tolerance; it is mindlessness.

From the question of immature ideas, it is not a very big jump to that of immoral ideas. If literature can morally affect the reader by sharpening awareness of human experience, how should one evaluate a poem that does the opposite—confuses the reader and encourages, say, fraud or racism? Granted that few poems come before the public that convey what most would term immoral ideas, and even fewer endure for long. But occasionally such a poem gains wide circulation—for example, canto 35 of Ezra Pound's *Cantos*, which preaches anti-Semitism. Surely such poems or parts of poems should be heavily criticized for their themes. The tendency toward book burning is always a danger in such an endeavor, of course, but the alternative is unthinking acceptance of all ideas and the establishment of an artificial esthetic realm for poetry, a realm which is both safe and unimportant.

3

Versification
(rhythm, meter, rime, stanza forms, sonnets)

Unlike a grasp of the meaning of a poem, which is essential to anything like an appreciation, knowledge of its versification (or prosody) takes one beyond such simple enjoyment to a more-developed understanding and consequently to a much deeper appreciation. Versification, which constitutes the most formal element of a poem, would at one time have been seen as the vessel into which the content was poured, but such is no longer an acceptable view, for the New Criticism has insisted that form is inseparable from content, even that they are in fact the same.

There is a great deal of truth to the notion of indivisibility of content and form. A poem is a complicated construct with organic unity; that is, it shares the complexity of an organism rather than the relative simplicity of a machine with interchangeable parts. Form and content are therefore inextricably bound together; part of the meaning of a line, for example, is conveyed by the meter, and the meaning controls to an extent the metrical sound of the line. And yet, for the purpose of analysis, distinctions must be made; otherwise nothing more than a superficial knowledge of a poem would be possible. The literary critic largely responsible for the modern organic view, Samuel Taylor Coleridge, pointed out in chapter 14 of his *Biographia Literaria*, "The office of philosophical *disquisition* consists in just *distinction*; while it is the privilege of the philosopher to preserve himself constantly aware, that distinction is not division" (Coleridge's italics).

RHYTHM

Rhythm is the most elemental fact about the sound of language in movement, and, as such, it is very difficult to define beyond that simple statement. Rhythm is often said to be a matter of regularity, but as I. A. Richards argues in *Practical Criticism* (1929), even that is doubtful. Any and all language in movement can be said to have rhythm, even the language of a police report or the list of ingredients on a bottle of cough syrup, although in the latter cases we are not likely to describe the movement as rhythmical. In short, defective rhythm still is rhythm. Yet it is only when we are pleased by linguistic movement that we use the term *rhythmical*; since pleasure is so much a part of the poetic experience, it isn't difficult to believe that, when we discuss the rhythm of a passage, we usually mean the pleasing rhythm we find there.

Free Verse

It would be hard to find much regularity in free verse, one of the most popular forms of versification today. In fact, the regularity of meter is precisely what *free verse* is *free* of. It has no pattern of stressed syllables, no appreciably recurrent rhythm from line to line or from stanza to stanza. The opening of Robert Lowell's "Grandparents" should convey the difference, for the first line is perfectly metrical, with every other syllable stressed (iambic pentameter), and the lines which follow are not:

> They're altogether otherworldly now,
> those adults champing for their ritual Friday spin
> to pharmacist and five-and-ten in Brockton.

Lines 2 and 3, like line 1, are rhythmical, but, unlike line 1, they are not metrical; that is, the last two lines flow, but the stressed and unstressed syllables do not fall into a regular pattern. If you set your mind and ear to it, you should be able to tell the difference.

Free verse does, however, share with metrical verse the use of the line as a unit. This shared use may not seem like much in view of the more elemental difference between the two kinds of verse, but it allows the free-verse poet to use the line breaks, pauses, and line lengths for special effects in much the same way a metrical poet would. For example, the isolation by Lowell of the two words "Never again" in the beginning line of the last section of the same poem allows him to emphasize them—as well as the finality they convey through their sense—and thus break with what goes before and prepare for the emotional outburst that follows. Free-verse poets may also use rime, as Lowell does in this poem, but most often they do not.

Prose Poetry

Prose poems, which are a more recent development, are distinguishable from free verse by the absence of the line as a unit; in fact, they are printed on the page as prose would be. But the rhythm of prose poetry is more prominent than that of most prose. For example, take the beginning of "The Aliens" by W. H. Auden:

> Wide though the interrupt be that divides us, runers and counters, from the Old World of the Plants, all capped in a tolerant silence, where, by the grace of chlorophyll, few of them ever have taken life and not one put a skeptical question, we nod them as neighbours, who, to conclude from the friendly response to the gardeners' handling, like to be given the chance to get more than a self-education.

Here the cadence, the rhythm, is quite prominent and pleasing, much more so than that of most prose. On the other hand, not only does prose have its own rhythms, but occasionally, when the context warrants, the rhythms of a passage of prose can surpass those of prose poetry and free verse and have all the regularity of metrical verse, as this short passage from the second chapter of Herman Melville's novel *Moby Dick* demonstrates: "The universe is finished; the copestone is on; and the chips were carted off a million years ago."

METER

Meter itself is often seized upon as that element which decisively separates poetry from prose, a criterion that would have been safe enough before Walt Whitman and other nineteenth-century poets developed free verse, but certainly not today, as we have already seen. Meter, nevertheless, has by no means been replaced by free verse; meter presents too many advantages to the poet ever to be discarded for good.

Meter is simply a more regular, controlled rhythm than the other verse forms we've just looked at, although even in metrical verse, meter and rhythm are distinguishable (the meter is the means, rhythm the end). Something like a scale exists, with increasingly prominent rhythms the closer you get to metered verse:

normal conversation	→ prose →	prose poetry	→ free verse →	metered verse

As conversation grows more intense or emotional, it tends to become increasingly rhythmical and emphatically stressed. Prose, moreover, can be very unrhythmical in the hands of the inexperienced; on the other hand, as we've seen, it can at moments outdo rhythmically both typical prose poetry and free verse. And yet as Karl Shapiro and Robert Beum point out in their *A Prosody Handbook* (1965), at the other end of the scale, meter that is *too* regular can seem decidedly unrhythmical. But in general the sliding scale is valid and may be helpful in understanding what the terms should convey.

Accentual meter, with its pattern of stressed and unstressed syllables, is a natural form for English poetry to take, even though it may seem artificial. For English is a stressed language; in any sentence some syllables receive more emphasis than others. Other languages have different characteristics and consequently different metrical forms, different ways of measuring the sounds; classical Greek and Latin use quantitative measure—long and short vowels occur in regular patterns; French poets use syllabic verse, which merely has a fixed number of syllables per line.

To point up the naturalness of accentual meter to English, it is only necessary to quote an experiment by an English poet in one of the other forms. Robert Southey tried quantitative verse in his *A Vision of Judgement:*

'Twas at the sober hour when the light of day is receding
And from surrounding things the hues wherewith day has
    adorn'd them
Fade, like the hopes of youth, till the beauty of earth is de-
    parted:
Pensive, though not in thought, I stood at the window, behold-
    ing

Mountain and lake and vale; the valley disrobed of its ver-
dure. . . .

There are a number of reasons, besides the accentual nature of English, why such verse doesn't work; one is that
the length of vowels in English tends to be uncertain. Syllabic verse has also been attempted in English, but the
effort to hold down the natural stresses of English while
counting the number of syllables doesn't really succeed,
even in otherwise successful syllabic poems such as Dyl-
an Thomas's "Poem in October." Rhythm will out, and,
in English, mere syllable counting becomes a game.

Metrical Feet

Actually, all English metered verse is syllabic as well
as accentual (or stressed). The shortest unit is the *foot*,
which consists of a fixed number of syllables, depending
on the kind of foot.

The *iambic* foot is the standard foot in English poetry;
it contains an unstressed syllable followed by a stressed.
The foot is marked in various ways, the stressed almost
always by a slant mark, the unstressed by a short or long
sign or a dot: tŏdáy, tōdáy, tòdáy.

Iambic meter provides a natural rhythm, close to conversation at its most intense; it is especially appropriate
to serious poetry, such as Arnold's "Dover Beach":

> Tȟe séa / ĭs cálm / tŏníght,
> Tȟe tíde / ĭs fúll, / tȟe móon / líes fáir
> Ŭpón / tȟe stráits. . . .

Once a metrical pattern such as iambic is set up by a
poet, any other foot is called a *substitution*. The other
two-syllable feet in English, the *trochee*, the reverse of
the iamb (névěr), and the *spondee*, with two stressed syllables (físhwífe), are most frequently used as substitute

feet in an iambic poem, although occasionally a poet will use trochaic meter as the basis for a poem—for example, William Blake's "The Tyger":

> Týgĕr, / týgĕr, / búrnĭng / bríght
> Iń thĕ / fórĕsts / óf thĕ / níght
> Whát ĭm / mórtăl / hánd ŏr / eýe
> Cŏuld fráme / thy feár / fŭl sým / mĕtríe?

Even here, however, the poet resorts to an unusual one-syllable foot at the end of the first three lines, which foot, being stressed, gives the lines a strong iambiclike ending; and then he uses straight iambic meter in the fourth line. Trochaic meter is unusual enough to be highly emphatic and thus to become rather monotonous in large doses.

As for the *spondee* (two evenly stressed syllables), some prosodists, such as Yvor Winters, insist that it doesn't really exist, that no two syllables ever receive the same stress, that one syllable will always receive the heavier stress. Indeed, there are often stressed syllables that are relatively more lightly stressed than others (and these are sometimes marked by a double slant line), as in the beginning of line 3 of "Dover Beach," quoted above. It might have been better scanned as "Ŭpón thĕ stráits." Such relative stresses have been known to complicate the scansion of poems, but they also provide variety to meter, thus avoiding the monotony of a too-regular beat.

The only other foot in much use in English is the *anapest*, which is a three-syllable foot, two unstressed syllables followed by a stressed (ĭntrŏdúce). By itself, anapestic meter is bouncy, so that it is especially suitable for comic poetry, or at least verse of a lighthearted sort. Even a sad subject can succumb to the tripping meter, as witness the opening of " 'Tis the Last Rose of Summer" by Thomas Moore:

'Tĭs thĕ lást / rŏse ŏf súm / mĕr, lĕft blóom / ĭng ălóne;
All hĕr lóve / lў cŏmpán / iŏns ăre fád / ĕd ănd góne;
Nŏ flówer / ŏf hĕr kínd / rĕd, Nŏ róse / bŭd ĭs nígh,
Tŏ rĕfléct / băck hĕr blúsh / ĕs ŏr gíve / sĭgh fŏr sígh.

But it is only fair to note that Moore's poem is also a song set to music, and so the lightness of the meter disappears when sung.

Mixed with iambic feet, however, anapestic meter, although light, does not cloy, at least in fairly small doses, as in e. e. cummings's "when faces called flowers":

whĕn fác / ĕš călled flów / ĕrs flōat oút / ŏf thĕ gróund
ănd bréath / ĭng ĭš wísh / ĭng ănd wísh / ĭng ĭš háv / ĭng—

Dactylic, the other three-syllable foot, is the reverse of anapestic, a stressed syllable followed by two unstressed (cértăĭnlў). It is rarely used in English poetry, almost never by itself.

Being syllabic, English metered verse is measured out in a pattern of so many feet per line. There are four common line lengths in English verse: *pentameter* with five feet per line, *tetrameter* with four, *trimeter* with three, and *dimeter* with two. These terms come up fairly often and are worth remembering. Longer lines—*hexameter* with six feet, *heptameter* with seven, *octameter* with eight—are seldom used in English, probably because such lines tend to split in two.

When iambic, the standard foot in English, comes five to a line, it forms the standard metrical line in English, *iambic pentameter,* which is the basis for blank verse and the heroic couplet (discussed below under "Rime"), as well as for most metered verse of a serious nature. *Iambic tetrameter,* its main competitor, tends to be a more facile meter with a lighter tone. Byron used it for *The Corsair:*

> As sneeringly these accents fell,
> On Selim's eye he fiercely gazed:
> That eye return'd him glance for glance
> And proudly to his sire's was raised. . . .

Andrew Marvell, however, used it for "To His Coy Mistress" with more subtlety:

> Had we but world enough, and time,
> This coyness, lady, were no crime.
> We would sit down, and think which way
> To walk, and pass our long love's day.

Iambic trimeter and dimeter are almost always combined with other line lengths, especially in stanzaic and ode forms.

Without rime, iambic pentameter becomes *blank verse*, which has been used in some of the greatest works of English poetry: Shakespeare's plays, Milton's *Paradise Lost*, and Wordsworth's *The Prelude*. But the form is also used in shorter poems, such as Celeste Wright's "Icy Harvest":

> To fill the storehouse on the bank a crew
> Were sawing channels in the frozen lake
> And pushing heavy blocks that bobbed along. . . .

Because of its relative proximity to conversation, blank verse is particularly well adapted to verse drama.

Scansion

Meter is one of the means that poets use to communicate; consequently, the metrical form provides us with a great deal of useful information when we set out to analyze a poem. The determination of the metrical form is called *scansion*, which, despite its relative simplicity, requires some practice.

The methods for scanning a poem are likewise simple. One can often determine the metrical form visually; if there are fourteen lines the poem is likely to prove a *sonnet*, fourteen lines of iambic pentameter with various rime schemes to be discussed later. If the lines of a poem seem of more-or-less-uniform length, the poem is probably either iambic pentameter or tetrameter, easily distinguished by counting the syllables if you cannot hear the difference. Similarly, a glance at a stanza form usually tells you whether it is, for example, a Spenserian stanza or a traditional ballad stanza, each with a predetermined metrical pattern and rime scheme. (Ballad form is discussed later in this chapter under "Stanza Forms.")

The second step is to mark the heavy stress in the line by reading it aloud or in your head. You should pronounce it, not to uncover the metrical pattern, a procedure which may cause you to misread the line, but rather to follow the sense of the line, allowing the metrical pattern to emerge naturally. Look especially for multisyllabic words (such as "storehouse"), which always carry the pronounced stress as given in the dictionary:

> Tŏ fíll thĕ stórehŏuse őn thĕ bańk ă créw. . . .

Notice that the most important parts of speech, nouns and verbs, receive most of the stresses, a normal occurrence, and that the meter itself seems to call for a secondary stress on the preposition "on," likewise very common. The remaining syllables are then marked as unstressed.

The third step is to divide the line into feet by looking for patterns of recognizable feet:

> Shĕ diéd / ĭn thĕ úp / stăirs béd / rŏom
> Bў thĕ líght / ŏf thĕ év' / nĭng stár. . . .

Notice here that, after the two iambic feet and one anapestic foot are separated in the first line, there is an unimportant unstressed syllable left at the end of the line. There is undoubtedly a name for such a foot in Greek, but the term and the foot are alike unimportant. What is important is to establish the metrical pattern of the poem as a whole. Look also for words that are commonly elided, such as interesting or evening; the missing syllable will of course affect the meter. If you are dealing with a stanzaic poem and the meter is difficult to scan, try more than one stanza to determine the pattern. If there is no discernible metrical pattern, then the poem is most likely written in free verse:

    those adúlts chámping for their rítual Fríday spín. . . .

The stresses are marked here only to show their irregular pattern, for of course free verse, being without meter, doesn't scan. Free verse normally has an irregular number of syllables per line as well.

Besides the bars that mark off metrical feet, double bars are sometimes used to show the position of the rhetorical pause within or at the end of the line, called a *caesura*. Especially important in such compact forms as the heroic couplet, caesuras provide another means of varying the rhythm of a poem, since the poet can position them in different places in the lines:

    Peace to all such! // but were there One whose fires
    True Genius kindles, // and fair Fame inspires,
    Blest with each talent // and each Art to please,
    And born to write, // converse, // and live with ease:
    Should such a man, // too fond to rule alone,
    Bear, // like the *Turk*, // no brother near the throne. . . .

               Alexander Pope, Epistle to Dr. Arbuthnot

Iambic pentameter? Mixed anapestic iambic tetrameter and trimeter? Quantitative verse? All of these terms are as valuable as any other terms—no more. They allow you to talk about the form of a poem, to describe it and analyze it. But they are not ends in themselves. In the study of English literature and of the humanities in general, there are few certainties, almost no 1, 2, 3s to rest secure upon. Metrical scansion often appears to provide such security, but one should resist the temptation. You could easily begin to care more about the metrics of the poem than about the poem itself.

One of the benefits accruing from a knowledge of metrical forms is the capacity to understand a large range of poetic techniques otherwise inaccessible, since, because of its regularity, meter usefully supports the meaning and emotions of a poem, especially where substitutions in feet occur. Usually, whatever variation from the norm has been set up tends to emphasize certain key words. In line 7 of "Dover Beach," for example, the substitution of a trochaic foot "Only" for the expected iambic at the beginning of the line tends to make the word more ominous, thus preparing the reader for the radical change in tone from "Sweet is the night-air!" to the sound of the surf which suggests the "human misery" that is central to the rest of the poem.

Substitutions can also be used for more elaborate effects where sound echoes sense. In the same poem (lines 3–4) occurs the sentence:

> . . .   ón thĕ Frénch coást / thĕ líght
> Gleáms aňd / iš goňe. . . .

The word "light," occurring as it does at the end of the line, receives a heavier-than-normal stress, and it is followed (over the line break) by the substitution of a trochee with a heavy first stress on "Gleams," followed by two weak unstressed syllables ("and is") and then the stressed "gone." I submit that the beam from a lighthouse follows temporally the same pattern, with the beam visible as it swings through the sea mist, suddenly bright as the light hits the viewer directly, and then dimming as it sweeps away.

Still another use of meter is to contrast it with the sense of the poem for effect. In "Death in Leamington," for instance, the death of the old woman is reported in the first stanza with a kind of bouncy, lighthearted rhythm set up by the anapestic-iambic meter:

> She died in the upstairs bedroom
> By the light of the ev'ning star
> That shone through the plate glass window
> From over Leamington Spa.

The sprightly rhythm contrasted with the serious subject aptly conveys the point of the poem: that the nurse, who enters a stanza later, displays exactly that contradiction in her attitude toward her patient.

Students often ask at this point whether the effects here ascribed to Matthew Arnold and John Betjeman are deliberate or merely accidental. Without attempting to probe the minds of poets past or present, it is enough to answer that poetry is an art and a craft, both of which when referred to a poet presuppose high verbal skills and intelligence. Such being the case, there is no reason to suppose that anything that happens in a poem is accidental, even though at times analysis can be too persistent and thus require impossibly complicated decisions on the part of the poet and leave little room for his unconscious mind or merely for happy chance. It is not always easy to decide where to draw the line.

Reading Poetry

Scansion is not the only technique required of readers set on getting the most out of poetry; many have considerable difficulty reading poetry properly. The two extremes often encountered are, on the one hand, a mechanical reading, especially of metered verse—where an attempt is made to make the meter more obvious—and, on the other, a dramatic reading in which the reader embellishes the sound of the poem with special emphases and flourishes. Anyone who has ever witnessed a typical Scotsman reading Robert Burns's "Tam O'Shanter" will know the full range of special effects possible.

What is needed is something in between a metronome and histrionics—what could be called a natural reading. If nothing else comes from a study of versification, at least one should be convinced that good poetry avoids the monotony of a heavy, unvaried beat. At the same time, poets worthy of the name are craftsmen who build into their poems the effects they desire. If a poem is read simply, with attention paid to its rhetorical meaning and punctuation, it should come across as intended. The only thing to remember beyond that is to pause slightly at the end of each line of metered or free verse, because the line constitutes an audial as well as a visual unit.

RIME

The remainder of versification consists of rime and the stanza forms constructed of rime. *Rime* is a poetic device, whereby the sound of one or more stressed syllables is repeated. It is often used along with meter and has consequently been popularly considered an elemental part of poetry, even though, as we have seen, the *blank* in *blank verse* denotes that it has no rime, while the *free* in *free verse* allows the poet the option of using rime.

Rime can take two forms, internal or terminal. *Internal* rime is most often part of a stanzaic pattern (as in line 5 of "when faces called flowers": "yes the pretty birds frolic as *spry* as can *fly*"), but it can also be used individually for emphasis. In "Grandparents," in the final, highly emotional section, internal rime occurs in the second line, "to *walk* there, *chalk* our cues," where it acts as part of the buildup of intensity by bringing an extra-heavy stress to the two words. But most rime is *terminal*; that is, it occurs at the end of the lines, in which case it is called simply *rime*.

The poverty of rime in English is well known; compared to an inflected language like Italian, with its many identical vowel endings, English presents a major challenge to a poet. Perhaps largely because of that poverty, English poets from at least the time of William Blake in the late eighteenth century have used rimes that are only close in sound, called variously *half-rime, approximate rime,* or *slant rime.* Examples from "Grandparents" are "gone" / "own," "cloth" / "both," and "spin" / "span." Half-rime, because of the unexpected disparity in sound, calls attention to the second rime-word and can therefore be used to emphasize that word.

More difficult than normal rime, on the other hand, is so-called *feminine* rime, which rimes on two or more syllables, always with the stress on other than the final syllable. The effect is usually to bring attention to the artificiality of the rime, the gross manipulation of sounds, and thus to produce a comic effect. Byron uses feminine rime throughout his comic epic *Don Juan;* some are outrageous:

> But—Oh! ye lords of ladies intellectual,
> Inform us truly have they not hen-peck'd you all?

Masculine rime is much more common and usually involves only one syllable, although when more than one syllable is involved it is only necessary that the final syllables are stressed, so that the lines involved end with strength:

> The farm's my own!
> Back there alone. . . .

Rime can fall into any number of patterns. The technique for reporting the pattern, or rime scheme, of a poem is to assign a letter to each rime sound; the rime scheme of "Death in Leamington" would thus be *a b c b.* Some prosodists prefer to assign *x* to nonrimed words (thus we would have here, instead, *x a x a*), but no indication is thereby given of how many nonrimed endings in a long poem are involved, and the other method is less trouble. Rime schemes can be very loose, as in the first section of "Dover Beach": *a b a c d b d c e f c g f g.* Rime can also be set up between fixed lines of stanzas, rather than within each stanza, as in "when faces called flowers," where the first, fifth, and sixth lines rime only between stanzas. But it is doubtful whether the sound effects of rime can function with such a distance between them.

More conventional rimes occur between adjacent or alternate lines. The couplet is one of the more common rime forms, especially iambic-tetrameter or iambic-pentameter couplets. Sometimes the idea and the rhythm are carried over (or *run on*) from one couplet to the next; such couplets are called *open:*

> Thou art not, Penshurst, built to envious show,
> Of touch or marble; nor canst boast a row
> Of polished pillars, or a roof of gold;
> Thou hast no lantern, whereof tales are told,
> Or stair, or courts; but stand'st an ancient pile,
> And, these grudged at, art reverenced the while. . . .

> *Ben Jonson, "To Penshurst"*

If, on the other hand, a couplet contains a complete idea and ends with a distinct pause or a complete end-stop, it is called *closed:*

> Such was that happy garden-state,
> While man there walked without a mate:

After a place so pure and sweet,
What other help could yet be meet!
But 'twas beyond a mortal's share
To wander solitary there:
Two paradises 'twere in one
To live in paradise alone.

Andrew Marvell, "The Garden"

Closed or open, iambic-pentameter couplets are known as *heroic couplets*; because of compactness, especially when closed, the heroic couplet is peculiarly adapted to satire and was used extensively by John Dryden and Alexander Pope. There was also a good deal of experimentation in the early nineteenth century in using the open heroic couplet for narrative purposes.

STANZA FORMS

Rime is a property of most if not all stanza forms, and probably the major use of rime is in stanzas. A *stanza* can be defined as a structured form which repeats fairly strictly the same pattern of meter and rime, and often even the same series of words, called a *refrain*. An example of stanza form is e. e. cummings's "when faces called flowers," which uses a very elaborate series of repetitions of rime, meter, and syntax and a refrain that is only slightly varied. Some prosodists allow any fairly regular grouping of lines, rimed or otherwise, to be called stanzas, but the term soon begins to lose the function of a term, that is, to distinguish one thing from another. It is preferable to call the divisions in a poem like "Icy Harvest" sections or verse paragraphs.

The most frequently used stanza form is the *quatrain*, which consists of four lines, usually rimed alternately. Perhaps the prototype of the quatrain is the traditional *ballad* stanza, which rimes the second and fourth lines of iambic trimeter but not the first and third lines of iambic tetrameter (a b c b, 4 3 4 3):

> There lived a wife at Usher's Well
> And a wealthy wife was she;
> She had three stout and stalwart sons
> And sent them o'er the sea.

"Death in Leamington" uses a variation of the traditional ballad stanza, exchanging anapestic feet for iambic quite liberally.

Poets seem to delight in using traditional stanzaic forms with complicated rime schemes despite the paucity of rimes in English. Perhaps the most difficult is the nine-line *Spenserian* stanza, with the rime scheme *a b a b b c b c c* connecting eight lines of iambic pentameter and a final *alexandrine* (six iambic feet). Devised by Edmund Spenser for *The Fairie Queene*, the Spenserian stanza was used fairly extensively by mid-eighteenth-century poets and later by John Keats for his "Eve of St. Agnes" and by Byron for his longer *Childe Harold's Pilgrimage*:

> A gentle Knight was pricking on the plaine,
> Ycladd in mightie armes and silver shielde,
> Wherein old dints of deepe wounds did remaine,
> The cruell markes of many a bloudy fielde;
> Yet armes till that time did he never wield:
> His angry steede did chide his foaming bitt,
> As much disdayning to the curbe to yield:
> Full jolly knight he seemed, and faire did sitt,
> As one for knightly giusts and fierce encounters fitt.

Edmund Spenser, The Faerie Queene, *I. i. 1*

The Spenserian stanza is adequate for description or reflection, although the temptation to pad out stanzas is great; but it is not especially useful for narrative because of the constant end-stopping effect of the alexandrines. The fact that Spenser himself used it successfully is a measure of his genius. Most writers of long poems in Spenserians tend eventually to run-on stanzas to keep the story going.

Other traditional stanzas have been imported from Italy. The *ottava rima* is eight lines of iambic pentameter rimed *a b a b a b c c*. Byron used the form in his comic masterpiece *Don Juan*, where the couplet at the end was often used with devastating effect:

> No doubt this patience, when the world is damning us,
> Is philosophic in our former friends;
> 'Tis also pleasant to be deem'd magnanimous,
> The more so in obtaining our own ends;
> And what the lawyers call a '*malus animus*'
> Conduct like this by no means comprehends:
> Revenge in person's certainly no virtue,
> But then 'tis not *my* fault, if *others* hurt you.

Ottava rima was also used very successfully by William Butler Yeats in short but serious poems, such as "Sailing to Byzantium." *Terza rima*, three-line stanzas with interlocking rime (*a b a b c b c d c*, etc.) is the form of Dante's *Divine Comedy*; Shelley used the form in his "Ode to the West Wind."

SONNETS

Another import from Italy, the sonnet, is not a stanza form but a poem in its own right, even though sonnets have often been used by poets in loose "sonnet sequences." *Sonnets* consist of fourteen lines of iambic pentameter with two major kinds of structure and rime scheme. The *Italian*, or *Petrarchan*, sonnet is written in two sections, sometimes so printed on the page: eight lines (*a b b a a b b a*) called the *octave* and six lines (*c d*

e c d e, c d c d e e, or some other variation) called the
sestet. The octave presents a subject or a problem; the
sestet offers a comment or a solution:

COMPOSED UPON WESTMINSTER BRIDGE, SEPTEMBER 3, 1802

Earth has not anything to show more fair:
Dull would he be of soul who could pass by
A sight so touching in its majesty:
This City now doth, like a garment, wear
The beauty of the morning; silent, bare,
Ships, towers, domes, theatres, and temples lie
Open unto the fields, and to the sky;
All bright and glittering in the smokeless air.
Never did sun more beautifully steep
In his first splendour, valley, rock, or hill;
Ne'er saw I, never felt, a calm so deep!
The river glideth at his own sweet will:
Dear God! the very houses seem asleep;
And all that mighty heart is lying still!

William Wordsworth

The other sonnet form is the *English,* or *Shakespearean,*
sonnet which consists of three quatrains (*a b a b*) and a
concluding couplet. The structure tends to present three
ideas or images in the three quatrains, along with a comment in the couplet. Perhaps the best-known example of
this form is Shakespeare's Sonnet 73:

That time of year thou mayst in me behold
When yellow leaves, or none, or few, do hang
Upon those boughs which shake against the cold,
Bare ruin'd choirs, where late the sweet birds sang.
In me thou see'st the twilight of such day
As after sunset fadeth in the west;

Which by and by black night doth take away,
Death's second self, that seals up all in rest.
In me thou see'st the glowing of such fire,
That on the ashes of his youth doth lie,
As the death-bed whereon it must expire,
Consum'd with that which it was nourished by.
This thou perceiv'st, which makes thy love more strong,
To love that well which thou must leave ere long.

Of the two sonnet forms the Italian has been used more extensively, perhaps because the structural division is more suitable to such a short form. Poets, however, have been known to adapt that structure freely for their own purposes. More English poets have undoubtedly tried their hand at the sonnet than at any other poetic form. It seems to present a challenge few can resist.

Knowledge of versification gives us most of the "vital statistics" of a poem. All the terminology presented in this chapter provides a way of describing the formal properties of a poem quickly; understood properly and with some experience of poetry in hand, such information can tell you some of the inherent properties of the poem, what to look for and what to expect, even at times what has been deliberately changed for effect.

From a superficial point of view, formal properties such as stanzas, line lengths, and meter may seem very artificial, but to a poet, form is a way of handling and controlling experience; and while in some sense all poetic forms are artificial, English poets have at least tended to use the most "natural" available, as iambic over trochaic meter, and the easiest, as simple rime schemes over more complex. But after all, art is not nature; it is a way of dealing with nature.

4

Imagery and Basic Figures of Comparison
(metaphor, simile, personification, allegory, symbolism)

The term *imagery* is problematic in that people use it to refer to a number of very different uses of language, some literal, some figurative. Perhaps by defining terms we can avoid, or at least lessen, the problem.

IMAGERY

Imagery is a literary device whereby sensory experience is rendered through words. For example, in the opening sentence of Arnold's "Dover Beach," we are presented immediately with a series of images of the scene before the speaker:

> The sea is calm tonight,
> The tide is full, the moon lies fair
> Upon the straits;—on the French coast the light
> Gleams and is gone; the cliffs of England stand,
> Glimmering and vast, out in the tranquil bay.

51

The poet then moves on to provide still more imagery as a way of giving immediacy to the opening section of the poem, which, indeed, sets the scene for the rest.

Imagery is a valuable asset to a poet, for if a sensory experience is brought clearly to mind for the readers, they can be involved more readily in the poem and thus gain some of the pleasure they expect from poetry. And yet it would be a mistake to assume that imagery is essential to poetry; there are successful poems that have no sensory imagery to speak of, such as Shakespeare's Sonnet 138:

> When my love swears that she is made of truth,
> I do believe her, though I know she lies,
> That she might think me some untutored youth,
> Unlearned in the world's false subtleties.
> Thus vainly thinking that she thinks me young,
> Although she knows my days are past the best,
> Simply I credit her false-speaking tongue:
> On both sides thus is simple truth suppressed.
> But wherefore says she not she is unjust?
> And wherefore say not I that I am old?
> Oh, love's best habit is in seeming trust,
> And age in love loves not to have years told.
> Therefore I lie with her and she with me,
> And in our faults by lies we flattered be.

Shakespeare shows us here that even so personal and concrete an experience as love can be rendered through abstractions, puns, and paradoxes. The mental images that poetic imagery evokes, moreover, may be idiosyncratic, providing us with that element of poetry that can be most personal, least easy to discuss. The first line of cummings's poem "when faces called flowers float out of the ground" presents to me a mental image of time-lapse photography, which tends to give a floating, though jerky, effect of flowers growing, but I have never encountered anyone else who experienced a similar effect from this line.

Another difficulty with the term is that it is often taken to refer only to visual images, probably because visual imagery is often so striking. In Arnold's "Dover Beach" we are confronted with the impressive image "moon-blanched land." Such a compound adjective as "moon-blanched" is easily passed over, but, on consideration, it summons up the desired mental image of a moonlit landscape. Sometimes when such scenes are experienced away from city lighting they can be seen almost as clearly as in daylight, but the color is missing; the effect is like watching a black-and-white movie. Because of the extraordinary vividness of such images as Arnold's, it is no wonder visual imagery holds a monopoly in our minds. Another probable reason for this emphasis is that people tend to visualize *all* the substantive words they run across.

In any event other kinds of imagery appear in poetry as well. In the same first section of "Dover Beach," the visual imagery is succeeded by images of smell (olfactory) with "sweet is the night air," and then the imagery is totally auditory after the appropriate direction (line 9):

> Listen! you hear the grating roar
> Of pebbles. . . .

Tactile imagery occurs in "Icy Harvest" in the description of the blocks of ice as "mealed with sawdust." Such imagery can be especially effective when an effect of shock is required, as later in the same poem:

> Thick tongues protruded; icicles encroached
> On mouths that often, warm and velvety,
> Had lipped the sugar from her proffered palm.

Images appealing to taste occur less frequently.

Synesthesia, which is a mixture of images from various senses, is a time-honored technique for suggesting the confusion of vision or dream, as it does in John Keats's "Ode to a Nightingale":

> I cannot see what flowers are at my feet,
> Nor what soft incense hangs upon the boughs,
> But, in embalmed darkness, guess each sweet. . . .

METAPHOR

As defined above, imagery involves the literal use of language. The descriptions are straightforward, conveyed in words that mean just what they say. But there is another use of language, the figurative, which conveys its meaning by using words in unusual ways—especially, but not solely, by comparing apparently dissimilar objects in order to show their similarity. Metaphors, similes, and personifications are just such figures of comparison, and, as if to confuse the term *imagery* further, these figures are also called *imagery*, whether or not they present sensory images. And so the literal and the figurative are confused under one term. In a minute, we shall see why.

Metaphors, in any case, always involve comparison. When in doubt, you can always ask, *What* is being compared to *what*? The comparison can be direct—"the boss is a bear"—or the property of one thing can be exchanged for that of another—"the boss growled at me." The two parts of a metaphor are often discussed in terms invented by I. A. Richards: the *tenor* signifies the thing to which the metaphor refers (the boss) and the *vehicle* signifies the metaphorical element applied (bear).

Metaphor is the main figure of comparison, so much so that it is often used to refer to all figures of speech, blurring distinctions still further. It is also sometimes considered to be *the* distinguishing poetic device—that is, to reach beyond the purpose of the comparison at hand and become *the* basis of all poetry. Just as the function of science is to analyze, to break things up in order to understand them, so poetry synthesizes, shows us the basic similarity of things—ultimately, the unity of all things.

Certainly the compactness of poetry draws attention to itself and allows for the use of more metaphors than prose can accommodate, but metaphors do occur in prose, just as they appear in everyday conversation of any interest. What are called *dead metaphors* indicate how natural metaphors are to language; after a while such metaphors as "the arm of a chair" or "a flower bed" lose their figurative status from frequent use and become literal images. We no longer are even aware that such phrases were once metaphorical until that is pointed out.

In poetry, metaphors can often be quite subtle, the comparison all but overlooked by the casual reader. In "Death in Leamington," it is only the unusual choice of words that points us to an underlying metaphor:

> Beside her the lonely crochet
> Lay patiently and unstirred. . . .

Alerted by the peculiar modifiers, we can discern that the crochet on the bed, lying "patiently and unstirred," is being subtly compared to a lapdog, the sort that is kept by old women. As a lifeless object identified with a live one, the crochet is thus a contrast to the nurse, who is alive but really "dead." The metaphor surfaces only for a moment, but it is there nonetheless and serves a purpose.

Most poetic metaphors are more obvious and functional. In line 2 of "Grandparents," the metaphor involved in "those adults champing for their ritual Friday spin" compares the grandparents in their impatience to horses, relying on the metaphorical cliché "champing at the bit" for the effect. There are also metaphors which are strung out, with the comparison made between more than two points of the things compared. Such an *extended* metaphor occurs in "Icy Harvest," with the grain-harvest metaphor of the title continued in "storehouse," "ice-crop," and "garnered up" and even suggested by "mealed."

In the hands of a skilled poet, a metaphor can be extended further into what was known in the seventeenth century as a *conceit* (see John Donne's "The Flea"). When a poet is careless, a metaphor can be extended clumsily, so that the points of comparison between the tenor and vehicle protrude in what has been described as "a metaphor crawling on all fours":

> Oh, weep for Adonais!—The quick Dreams,
> The passion-winged Ministers of thought,
> Who were his flocks, whom near the living streams
> Of his young spirit he fed and whom he taught
> The love which was his music, wander not. . . .

Percy Bysshe Shelley, Adonais, ll. 73–77

Here, besides some confusion in the metaphor, the original comparison becomes drawn out too far: a scene with Dreams/sheep drinking at the spirit/streams and being fed and entertained by love/music. The same effect of making the metaphor too material occurs in a line by Byron: "Perchance my heart and harp have lost a string."

Mixed metaphors, where the tenor or vehicle changes, can sometimes be very effective, as in the famous instance from *Hamlet*—"to take arms against a sea of trouble, / And by opposing end them," where the technique is used to convey the overwhelming difficulties Hamlet faces. But occasionally the mixture seems inadvertent, perhaps even caused by the rime scheme:

Nor is it discontent to keep the mind
Deep in its fountain, lest it overboil
In the hot throng, where we become the spoil
of our infection. . . .

Lord Byron, Childe Harold, *III, lxix*

SIMILE

At one time there was a useful distinction between metaphor and simile, the two main figures of comparison. *Metaphor*, a term which derives from the Greek word "to transfer," was applied to indirect comparisons only, where the property of one thing was transferred to or exchanged for that of another, as in the expression "the boss growled" (where growling, the property of an animal, is transferred to a man). *Similes* would then signify any direct comparison, whether stated or implied—"The boss is like a bear" and "The boss is a bear." For there is really no difference between the last two statements as far as meaning goes.

Today, however, the only accepted usage is that *simile* is a *stated* comparison, involving words such as *like, as if, than*. Metaphor, on the other hand, designates only *implied* comparisons. The modern distinction therefore is between apparent identity (metaphor) and expressed comparison (simile). Although this distinction is less useful than that between exchange and comparison, there is no resisting established usage: simile is stated comparison; metaphor, implied.

Like metaphor, simile at its best is not merely decorative but functions in the meaning of a poem. In Lowell's "Grandparents" we have two similes in a row:

Grandpa still waves his stick
like a policeman;
Grandmother, like a Mohammedan, still wears her thick
lavender mourning and touring veil. . . .

The points of comparison in both similes are clear enough and together they present us with a most "otherworldly" couple (line 1): a policeman with his nightstick and a Mohammedan in purdah. In "Death in Leamington," the old woman's fingers are described as "dead as the spoken word," a simile which prepares us for the nurse's "dead" words (and the speaker's subsequent comments) several stanzas later:

> And 'Tea!' she said in a tiny voice
> 'Wake up! It's nearly five.'
> Oh! Chintzy, chintzy cheeriness,
> Half dead and half alive!

If *imagery* as a term is often used to include figures of speech with or without concrete images, it is surely because so often concrete images and metaphors are combined. In the metaphor from "Grandparents," five light bulbs are said to "spider the billiards-table," presenting clearly the concrete image of the lights hanging from their wires while at the same time commenting ironically on the grandparents' holding "nature at a distance" by bringing in metaphorically the insect from nature. The simile (introduced by "as") at the end of "Dover Beach" likewise does double duty:

> And we are here as on a darkling plain
> Swept with confused alarms of struggle and flight,
> Where ignorant armies clash by night.

A visual and auditory image is presented to the reader, as well as a brilliant simile comparing modern purposeless civilization to a battlefield at night with its senseless slaughter and utter confusion.

In any event, the indeterminate use of the term *imagery* should keep us alert to problems. And since this usage is really more a matter of carelessness than established convention, perhaps by using *image* to signify a verbal presentation of a sensory experience and *metaphor* and *simile* to denote figures of comparison we can keep the terms better distinguished and therefore more useful.

Several kinds of metaphors present unique difficulties. *Personification*, which is the comparison of an abstraction or a nonhuman thing with a human by attributing to it human qualities, is a subspecies of metaphor. The danger in identifying personification is misapprehension about what constitute distinctly human qualities. For example, toward the end of "Icy Harvest" occurs the expression "Terror now gaped . . . ," which contains an abstraction, "Terror"—abstractions are the most obvious and frequent of personified tenors. But "gaped" is not a distinctly human activity; in fact in this sentence it refers to the gaping hole in the ice or the gaping mouths of the horses rather than a gaping mouth of a personified Terror (why would Terror be gaping in any event?). Often activities such as leaping, eating, or standing, which humans share with animals, are mistakenly seen as determining personification; figures based on these comparisons are simply metaphors.

Personification is sufficiently complicated to have been divided in two by Chester Chapin, a scholar of eighteenth-century English literature. In that era there was a great deal of what he denominated *allegorical* personification, which asks the reader to visualize a person, especially a personified abstraction. Such allegorical personifications are usually as elaborately described as the depictions in the allegorical paintings so popular in the period. Anger might be described as tearing out his hair or Sleep as having heavy eyelids.

The other kind of personification, called *rhetorical*,

resists visualization or at least does not encourage it, but rather acts as a kind of shorthand, or more economical manner of saying something. Instead of going into some length, for example, about the unhappy effects of the child's discovering the dead horses in "Icy Harvest," with the consequent loss of the joie de vivre and lightheartedness engendered by the earlier scene, Celeste Wright has the narrator state simply "Delight was murdered." There is no suggestion of a figure standing over Delight with a bloody knife; but there is concisely conveyed the powerful effect of the discovery.

ALLEGORY

Allegory is essentially a kind of extended metaphor whereby at least two levels of meaning are presented to the reader. Like metaphor, allegory presents a one-to-one relationship on each level between the tenor and the vehicle, such as that existing in Book 1 of the *Fairie Queene,* where in the moral allegory the Red Crosse Knight stands for holiness, the Palmer for reason (a guide in moral matters), and so on. But unlike metaphor, the purpose of the allegorical correlation is not to function as decoration or illumination but to provide a story on the literal level and an interpretation on another level.

Allegory doesn't, strictly speaking, exist in the sort of short poem dealt with in an introductory course; shorter poems more likely contain an extended metaphor. But a distinction set forth by C. S. Lewis in his *Allegory of Love* (1936) provides an excellent introduction to another device used by poets—symbolism.

SYMBOLISM

According to C. S. Lewis, allegory is a mode of expression (like metaphor), while symbolism denotes a mode of thought when used in its full and proper sense with regard to literature. There are, of course, other, nonliterary uses of the term *symbol*. In everyday life we might say that a final paycheck symbolizes the termination of a job, just as falling leaves symbolize the coming of the end of the year. In literature, we also speak of traditional or conventional symbols, such as a rose symbolizing love or sleep symbolizing death. But in most such instances, what is often called a symbol is really a mode of expression, not of thought; and the term *metaphor* is adequate to describe the usage. In the above examples, love is in fact implicitly being compared to a rose, sleep to death. In some exceptional instances, there does not, however, seem to be any direct comparison made, as in water "symbolizing" materialism for William Blake; but in any case a simple one-to-one relationship is set up. A symbol is sometimes even described as an extended metaphor— one that is repeated—or a metaphor without a stated tenor. Clearly on this level the term *symbol* has a limited usefulness and can even lead to confusion. And yet it is often difficult to avoid saying that something symbolizes something else and it would perhaps be pedantic not to use the expression, as long as you are aware of what you mean by it.

There is, however, another use for the term that draws on C. S. Lewis's view of it as a mode of thought. Lewis claimed that the background of literary symbolism is metaphysical—that is, that a true poetic symbolist sees the material world as a copy of a transcendent reality and attempts to approach that transcendent world by means of material symbols. The world to be approached can be, for example, the idealistic universe of Plato, or the Christian cosmos that partly evolved from it, or even a privately viewed transcendent reality, as those expressed by such modern poets as William Blake or William Butler Yeats. But that world must transcend the natural world.

A symbol may begin in a work by seeming to be a metaphor, but then the symbol—a thing or an action—leaves the one-to-one analogy of metaphor and allegory and begins to assume symbolic proportions. That is, the reader is no longer able to pin down exactly what such a symbol represents; indeed, symbols are valuable for their ability to go beyond discursive reason, and this transcending quality is what makes true symbols so difficult to discuss. You might even say that, if a symbol is fully discussable, then it isn't strictly a successful symbol, for the writer hasn't transcended logic to deal with the inexplicable.

William Wordsworth fairly early in his poetic career attempted to deal with the inexplicable, the inexpressible. In a passage in "Tintern Abbey" (1798), he tried to set forth what it was in nature that he was experiencing:

> And I have felt
> A presence that disturbs me with the joy
> Of elevated thoughts; a sense sublime
> Of something far more deeply interfused,
> Whose dwelling is the light of setting suns,
> And the round ocean and the living air,
> And the blue sky, and in the mind of man:
> A motion and a spirit, that impels
> All thinking things, all objects of all thought,
> And rolls through all things.

Readers may claim they know precisely what Wordsworth means, but it seems unlikely that Wordsworth himself did. William Empson, a New Critic well known for his study *Seven Types of Ambiguity* (1930), chose this passage as an example of ambiguity gone mushy, but what he didn't see is that Wordsworth, in his attempt to express the inexpressible, had merely stacked one vague, inadequate phrase upon another ("A presence," "a sense sublime," and so on). What he should have done was use a symbol.

A few years later, Wordsworth did exactly that. In *The Prelude* (1805) he described a mystical experience that occurred to him shortly after crossing a pass through the Alps:

The Brook and Road
Were fellow-travellers in this gloomy pass,
And with them did we journey several hours
At a slow step. The immeasurable height
Of woods decaying, never to be decayed,
The stationary blasts of waterfalls,
And every where along the hollow rent
Winds thwarting winds, bewildered and forlorn,
The torrents shooting from the clear blue sky,
The rocks that muttered close upon our ears,
Black drizzling crags that spake by the wayside
As if a voice were in them, the sick sight
And giddy prospect of the raving stream,
The unfettered clouds and region of the Heavens,
Tumult and peace, the darkness and the light—
Were all like workings of one mind, the features
Of the same face, blossoms upon one tree;
Characters of the great Apocalypse,
The types and symbols of Eternity,
Of first, and last, and midst, and without end.

Book 6, lines 553–572

Notice that in this passage there is not the same attempt to describe abstractly what it is Wordsworth is experiencing. There is instead the contrast of stasis and movement, "tumult and peace," and then the grand similes that bring the passage to an end and make it clear that there is more going on than mere natural description, that the scene itself is symbolic.

Literary symbols are easiest to discuss when they occur in long narrative works, such as *The Prelude* or Melville's *Moby Dick*, which concerns the great white whale, perhaps the most famous literary symbol of them all. It has been discussed by scholars at great length, but perhaps such symbols must be grasped the way they are created, intuitively.

Samuel Taylor Coleridge once argued that a successful literary symbol arises naturally out of a work; one never feels that it was worked up. In Larry McMurtry's novel *Horseman, Pass By* (from which the movie *Hud* was made), such a successful symbol occurs in an action that arises naturally out of the plot and sums it up brilliantly. When the shot rings out that kills the last of the longhorns, it reverberates through the story, symbolizing the death of honor, the West, the old man—all of these things and more. And it works as a symbol whether or not you are aware of it.

Perhaps the reason examples of literary symbols usually are taken from longer narrative works is that symbols need contexts; they must be prepared for. An exception to this statement would be the sort of poems produced by poets of the French Symbolist Movement and by those poets in other languages who were influenced by them, such as T. S. Eliot, William Butler Yeats, and Wallace Stevens in English. In many of their poems these poets attempted the use of symbols as modes of thought but in shorter forms. These short symbolic poems, however, are highly evocative and difficult to deal with and thus are no more likely to be found in an introductory course than long narrative poems that contain symbolism.

5

Diction
(connotation and denotation, collocation, allusion)

D*iction* is simply the choice of words a poet makes. But if simple to define, diction is perhaps the most important test of a poet, for the choice of words in poetry is anything but simple. It is all too easy for a poet to be too precise, stilted, too suggestive, sloppy.

CONNOTATION AND DENOTATION

There are two different aspects of diction, two different qualities inherent in words—denotation and connotation. The two are not always easily distinguished, but in general the denotation of a word is its primary, most literal meaning. *Denotation* is often said to be the dictionary meaning of a word, but given a large enough dictionary, the associations or suggestiveness—the connotations—of a word are also supplied to some extent. *Woman* is a fairly neutral word denoting a person of the feminine gender, but *lady* has certain connotations of quality, perhaps even of gentility, while *female* can connote certain unfavorable things, especially when used by some persons in some contexts.

A good deal of pleasure can be derived from detecting the apt denotative use of words, the precision of language in a poem, what the French call *le mot juste*—exactly the right word. It is present when you stop reading a poem and say to yourself, "This is the word that is wanted, and no other word would have done quite as well."

For example, in line 8 of "Icy Harvest"—"The sunshine twinkled on the floating ice"—"twinkled" denotes that exact kind of motion of light on ice that is beginning to melt, thus providing a hint of the disaster to come. "Plunging" in line 12 likewise denotes the precise action of the heavy draught horses falling through the ice. Several other words in the passage that follows ("buffeted," "encroached") are likewise worth comment for their precision, but in line 20 occurs the preeminent example. The horses' mouths are said to have "lipped" the sugar from her palm, not "licked," as perhaps one might have expected and a less alert poet have provided. It is, however, precisely the lips, not the tongue, that horses use in such eating.

More emphasis is usually placed on the *connotations*, the suggestiveness of words, possibly because of the richness such associations provide; and of course poetry is known for its verbal richness. William Empson, who celebrated the richness of poetic diction in his *Seven Types of Ambiguity* (1930), claimed that all good poetry has ambiguity of one sort or another, often relying on connotations of words.

At least we can be certain that most poets put the associations of words to good use. In "Death in Leamington," for example, the narrator describes the nurse in line

10 as entering "Breast high 'mid the stands and chairs," suggesting by "Breast high" a rather buxom woman, crisp and straight-spined. Later in the same poem (line 23), the arches from which the plaster drops are described as "Italianate," suggesting by their presence in the English climate a certain phoniness.

Some poets tend to stress the connotations of words. e. e. cummings very cleverly used connotations as if they were denotations in his characteristic technique of interchanging parts of speech. In the third line of each stanza of "when faces called flowers," for example, he relied on the negative connotations of the words to convey his meaning: "but keeping is downward and doubting and never. . . ."

Other poets who write without such disjunction of syntax often work almost exclusively by suggestion, as witness passages from the first two stanzas of Swinburne's "Before the Beginning of Years":

> Before the beginning of years
> There came to the making of man
> Time, with a gift of tears;
> Grief, with a glass that ran;
> Pleasure, with pain for leaven;
> Summer, with flowers that fell;
> Remembrance fallen from heaven,
> And madness risen from hell. . . .
>
> And the high gods took in hand
> Fire, and the falling of tears,
> And a measure of sliding sand
> From under the feet of the years. . . .

The words used are pleasant and poetical enough—time, pleasure, summer, remembrance—and the drift of the poem easy enough to follow, but not a great deal of denotative meaning is being conveyed. Such reliance on connotation can eventually sap language of meaning. As John Keats so aptly put it, "English must be kept up."

On the other hand, diction in the hands of a skillful poet is largely responsible for poetry's ability to convey much in little, to convey a lot of meaning with few words. The expression "glassy miles" in line 21 of "Icy Harvest" conveys a great deal, especially the adjective "glassy." The miles are of course glassy in the most obvious metaphorical way of being icy—translucent, hard, and shiny. But "glassy" conveys even more the fragile nature of the girl's world, the "miles" stretched before her, and seems more alien and strange as well.

Another, perhaps better, example of the skillful economy of diction occurs in lines 7–8 of "Grandparents," where the grandmother is described as wearing a "thick lavender mourning and touring veil." The combination of "mourning and touring" tells you a good deal about the grandmother, that she was of that sort of thrifty rich folk who get double duty from their possessions; in this case her veil is lavender, dark enough for a funeral, but unfunereal enough (unlike black) for automobile touring. One detail can thus quickly sketch-in a character in a short poem.

But the best example of economic diction, occurring in the same poem, turns on a single word. For by line 7 of the poem, the reader is told clearly but indirectly which of the two grandparents the boy had a close relationship with. If you read the lines closely you will detect that the speaker refers to the two grandparents in slightly but significantly different terms: one is the familiar "Grandpa," the other the formal "Grandmother." Thus, by the end of the second section, when Grandpa hides the stain on the billiards table from his wife, the reader is aware of the relationship between the three main characters. A novelist might be hard pressed to do as much in a chapter.

The indirection noticeable in the last few examples is another feature often found in poetic diction. An oblique expression found in the same poem provides an example: the speaker refers to his "throw-away and shaggy span of adolescence" (lines 4–5), the phrasing of which is evocative but difficult. "Shaggy" presents no major problem when associated with adolescence inasmuch as boys in their early teens are often unkempt, but "throw-away" requires more thought: it refers to the throwing away of clothes that no longer fit because of rapid growth in the early teens.

e. e. cummings made indirection a feature of his poetry. In line 12 of "when faces called flowers," we are told the birds "hover so she and so he," and we see that cummings means by the transfer of parts of speech that the birds are involved in courtship and mating. cummings also provides examples of how poets can deal with conventional or trite expressions, surprising the reader with the unexpected. In the same poem we have "fish," not lambs, gamboling (line 6), and instead of the expression "as high as [they] can fly" we are given unexpectedly "as spry as can fly" (line 5). By such devices as this, cummings manages to take so well-worn a genre as a hymn to spring and make it vital.

A poet's facility with language shows up also in puns and plays on words, which are simply other methods for providing verbal richness. In "Icy Harvest" the drowned horses are said to have "desperation frozen in their eyes" (line 17). Both senses of *frozen*—fixed and turned to ice—are clearly being used, and in the process the ghastly image of their wide, staring eyes is emphasized. In "Grandparents" the grandparents are described in the first line as being "altogether otherworldly now," with the "altogether" removing the sense from merely the outrageous appearance of the couple (commented on in the last chapter) and thus punning on "otherworldly," which also signifies that they are in the "other" world, or dead.

But to say as I did in opening this chapter that diction is *simply* the choice of words is a bit misleading, for, as with most literary terms, there are some qualifications and complexities to point out regarding the term *diction*. The first qualification is that diction is easily confused with certain figures of speech that are also mainly choices of expression, such as *circumlocution* (or periphrasis). Popular especially in the eighteenth century, circumlocution involves saying something in a roundabout way, usually to present it in a more favorable light, as with the euphemism *passed away* for *died*. Sometimes poets can obtain a sarcastic distance by using circumlocution; Philip Larkin, in his "Church Going," has the speaker ask sardonically whether after we have selected a few churches for display men will in future irreligious days "let the rest rent-free to rain and sheep?"—another way of saying "will they abandon them?" The closeness of circumlocution to diction should in any event be clear.

COLLOCATION

Another qualification to the term *diction* is that it often is made to refer not just to the choice of words but to their arrangement (or *collocation*) as well. Inverting a series of words ("To fill the storehouse on the bank a crew / Were sawing channels. . . .") is often spoken of as a matter of diction, perhaps because word choice and arrangement are both comprised under the term *style*. It is, however, preferable to speak of diction and collocation as two different elements.

ALLUSION

Beyond diction but allied to it is the poet's use of *allusion*—a word or, more usually, a phrase that draws the reader's memory to another context and by doing so expands the meaning of the new passage in which it occurs. Some allusions are directly literary, appealing verbatim to the reader's experience of another literary work. In line 13 of "Grandparents" we are told, "They're all gone into a world of light," an almost word-for-word rendition of the first line of a poem by Henry Vaughn, a seventeenth-century English poet and mystic. Vaughn's poem is a meditation on immortality, and consequently the allusion deepens the meaning of Lowell's poem, adding a mystical dimension.

A literary allusion unfamiliar to the reader can't of course work in the manner described above. If, however, the reader is supplied with annotations by the poet, as in T. S. Eliot's *The Waste Land*, or by scholars, as in the case of Ezra Pound's *Cantos*, the allusions can still function, but they can hardly function as well as they would if known and recalled by the reader. A reader's literary background can be invaluable from this point of view alone, the reading of new poems.

Other, nonliterary allusions are often quite fragmentary; some are merely distant echoes. In "Grandparents" the speaker loses control toward the end of the poem and addresses his deceased grandfather: "Have me, hold me, cherish me!" In the Christian wedding service occur the words "to have," "to hold," and "to cherish" as descriptive of the relationship between husband and wife. The echo suggests the depth of the speaker's relationship to his grandfather.

cummings's "when faces called flowers" contains a

biblical allusion as part of the refrain at the end of every stanza. The image of a mountain dancing occurs in the 114th Psalm, and the allusion makes the image joyful rather than silly. Less certain is an allusion in the last line of "Icy Harvest": "In the deceitful glitter of the sun." "Glitter" may also allude to a common saying, All that glitters is not gold, taken from Shakespeare's line in *Merchant of Venice* (II, vii, 65), "All that glisters is not gold." Such an echo, if it is not too farfetched, would reinforce the sentiment about nature's deceit, prominent at that point of "Icy Harvest."

The context on which an allusion draws need not be literary at all, as perhaps the last example demonstrates at one remove. Old sayings and conversational clichés, the more hackneyed the better, provide a fertile source of allusions. In "Grandparents" Lowell twice made subtle use of such expressions. In line 12 the speaker announces that "the nineteenth century, tired of children, is gone," drawing upon the Victorian dictum that "children should be seen and not heard" for its meaning, although here there is no allusion in the usual sense. When the speaker remarks in line 16 that he stays inside "and spoil[s] another season" we are probably not too far from the idiom of his grandmother trying to drive him outdoors. So too in "Icy Harvest" when we are told (line 5) that the ice is destined for "the great hotel," we can sense the awed attitude of the natives toward the resort; perhaps it is even the expression used by them.

And sometimes allusions can derive from a mere juxtaposition of details that finally add up to a specific reference, as takes place in the last section of "Dover Beach." The world stripped of illusions

> Hath really neither joy, nor love, nor light,
> Nor certitude, nor peace, nor help for pain. . . .

Since what the speaker is bemoaning are the qualities of life connected with a Christianity he sees as moribund, it is not surprising that many of the terms occur in Christian and specifically New Testament phrases: "I bring you tidings of great joy," "God is love," "I am the light of the world," "Peace I leave with you, my peace I give you." These phrases are not directly echoed, but surely they are audible, just barely, in the background.

Many of the examples given of diction and allusion ask a good bit of subtlety on the part of the poet and reader; some probably work on an unconscious level—perhaps even more effectively there. Others may be the result of chance. But subtlety and precision are the hallmarks of successful diction, especially from the point of view of a reader desirous of getting everything possible from a poem.

6

Tone and Intellectual Figures of Speech
(irony, hyperbole and understatement, paradox)

There is an intellectual side to poetry that goes beyond content into the formal elements of a poem, and this side requires a good deal of attention and thought. But it also pays disproportionately high rewards.

TONE

Of all the elements that go to make up a poem, tone is without doubt the most difficult to define, discuss, or discern in a poem. And since the meaning of a poem ultimately depends on the proper understanding of its tone, it can become the key to poetic analysis.

Tone is the attitude or ultimate intention of a poet as seen in what the speaker of the poem says and how it is said. The tone can be serious, lighthearted, scornful, delighted, tongue-in-cheek. The reader must keep an eye out for every indicator of tone in a poem—after a while doing so becomes more or less automatic. For, if one thinks, for example, that the tone of a poem is serious when in fact it is tongue-in-cheek, one will make nonsense of the poem.

Not every poem offers problems of tone. "Dover Beach" and "Icy Harvest" present no special problems of tone; they are both straightforward and serious in intent with nothing in them to mislead the reader into thinking otherwise. "when faces called flowers" and "Death in Leamington," however, are alike presented in a tripping iambic-anapestic meter that makes both sound lighthearted. But while cummings's poem is given over to a tone of enthusiastic delight—"it's april(yes,april; my darling)it's spring!"—Betjeman's is a bit more complicated. The metrical lightness contrasts with the subject of death to begin with; and the intrusion of the narrator in the fifth stanza ("Oh! Chintzy, chintzy cheeriness") should alert us to a more serious, more scornful tone, which in fact that metrical contrast helps to reinforce.

To demonstrate still further the difficulties of determining tone, let's examine two poems presented by a popular poetry handbook in discussing the subject.

THE VILLAIN

While joy gave clouds the light of stars,
    That beamed where'er they looked;
And calves and lambs had tottering knees,
    Excited, while they sucked;
While every bird enjoyed his song,
Without one thought of harm or wrong—
I turned my head and saw the wind,
    Not far from where I stood,
Dragging the corn by her golden hair,
    Into a dark and lonely wood.

W. H. Davies

APPARENTLY WITH NO SURPRISE

Apparently with no surprise
To any happy flower,
The frost beheads it at its play
In accidental power.

The blond assassin passes on,
The sun proceeds unmoved
To measure off another day
For an approving God.

Emily Dickinson

Both poems involve nature and a contrast between innocence and evil, as Laurence Perrine points out in *Sound
and Sense* (5th ed., 1977, p. 154). But the first, he argues,
has a tone of delight while the second has a tone of grim
horror. It would be worthwhile to read both poems closely
to see if you agree.

We can all agree, I believe, that "The Villain" begins
with a joyful tone, with delightful images of clouds and
young animals; but that the final metaphor of violence
(the wind "dragging the corn by her golden hair, / Into a
dark and lonely wood") is meant to be pleasantly fanciful
is hard to swallow. If the image were meant to be merely
fanciful, the poet would surely not have had the wood
"dark and lonely." Only by calling rape euphemistically
"some unmentionable deed" in his analysis, moreover,
does Perrine make his reading seem plausible.

It is the approval of God in the last line of Dickinson's
"Apparently with No Surprise" that seems to lead to Perrine's finding its tone, on the other hand, one of horror.
That the assassin—the frost—is described as "blond,"
connoting "innocence and beauty," he finds ironic, but I
believe the connotations are rather a tip-off to another,
quite different tone and meaning.

For both poems have, I believe, a common purpose of attacking the human sentimentalizing of nature and natural processes, although the two poems set about their purpose in very different ways. In Davies's poem, the speaker is at first presented as naive; he believes that the birds sit and sing "without one thought of harm or wrong," even though he is presumably aware that they would fly off if he approached them. At just that moment, the speaker looks over and sees the wind, one of the most violent and destructive forces in nature, bending the grain; suddenly he realizes his mistake and conveys his new awareness through the rape metaphor.

In Dickinson's poem, on the other hand, the speaker is being deliberately ambiguous and works with the sentimental assumptions of many readers. In contrast to the normal human surprise at the life and death process, the flower is seemingly not surprised, and the beheading is described as "accidental" in line 4, not malignant. A play on words, moreover, occurs in line 6 ("proceeds unmoved"), hardly what one would expect in a grim poem. Finally, we are told that God, who presumably approves of the fall of sparrows and all the natural processes He set into motion, approves of the death of the flower. It is only we humans who don't understand nature and, like the speaker in the other poem, need to sentimentalize it. In both cases, the readings I have presented seem to me more likely, to have fewer problems and inconsistencies, and, thus read, the poems seem more interesting to boot.

It is, I believe, the euphemism supplied by Perrine for the first poem and his all-too-human predisposition in the case of the second that led to their being misread—that is, if I am correct. Two points would, in any event, be worth seizing from the disagreement. One is the ease with which a person can mistake the tone of a poem, including someone who has written an introductory poetry text (one of us is wrong). The other point is that questions of tone in any case are not up for grabs. Each poem has a context with details that one must scrutinize to determine its tone, though one should remain open to disagreements with his own understanding of that tone.

Persona

One problem related to tone that tends to seduce the unwary involves the speaker, or narrator, of a poem. Poets tend to use what is called a *persona* (Latin for "mask") when they compose a poem, a fictitious character that suits the point they are trying to make. In fact, the reader should *never* assume that the speaker of the words of a poem is the poet. It is always better to use the terms *the speaker* or *the narrator* instead of *the poet*, unless you are referring to the guiding mind behind the entire poem, including the creation of the speaker.

It is easy enough to keep such a warning in mind when dealing with drama, for there is clearly a group of characters, too many to all represent the author; but even so one often hears Shakespeare taken as the possessor of some sentiment delivered by one of his characters: "As Shakespeare in *King Lear* so aptly insisted, 'Ripeness is all.' " Some Romantic poets even seem to insist on their identification with the speakers of their poems; Wordsworth addresses his sister Dorothy in verse and Byron his daughter Ada. But one should be wary and never make the consequent assumptions. There is probably at least some difference between the actual personality of a poet and the speaker deliberately created for public consumption. Even when you write a private letter to a friend, are you really being you, or are you creating an image of yourself you prefer?

IRONY

The use of a persona brings us naturally to the question of irony, where a poet is clearly not being himself. *Irony* is a figure of speech in which the real meaning of the poet is different from what is stated—sarcasm is simply a crude form of irony, for example. In literature, verbal irony is most often more refined and complicated; it is in fact an intellectual device that asks a good deal of effort from the reader. One must be alert to the indications that what is being said is intended to carry a contrary meaning, and the many anecdotes about readers who have taken outrageous irony at face value would suggest that irony is easily missed. Thom Gunn's narrator remarks in the opening of "Autumn Chapter in a Novel":

> Through woods, Mme Une Telle, a trifle ill
> With idleness, but no less beautiful,
> Walks with the young tutor. . . .

But we are not to miss the nuance that she is only a "trifle" ill, that the illness is really ennui, the chronic French disease of the "beautiful people," and that she didn't allow the "illness" to affect her beauty. Gunn's narrator is being ironic: Mme Une Telle is not ill at all.

Verbal irony is so denominated to distinguish it from irony of situation, where the events in a poem turn out unexpectedly and inappropriately (at least in one sense). For instance, in Shelley's "Ozymandias," we are presented with the egotistical rantings of a once powerful Egyptian king sculpted on a broken pedestal: "My name is Ozymandias, king of kings: / Look on my works, ye Mighty, and despair!" The irony, which could be cut with a chain saw, is contained in the conclusion:

> Nothing beside remains. Round the decay
> Of that colossal wreck, boundless and bare
> The lone and level sands stretch far away.

Irony of situation is often more subtle than this example, but it is usually not as difficult to spot as verbal irony; in any case it is not so important for questions of tone, even though a twist at the end of a poem can sometimes cause you to reread the work in a different light.

HYPERBOLE AND UNDERSTATEMENT

Hyperbole (or exaggeration) is one type of verbal irony; *understatement* another. Both are ironic in not saying what is actually meant: in the case of hyperbole more is said; with understatement, less. In Andrew Marvell's "To His Coy Mistress," the speaker addresses his love hyperbolically:

> I would
> Love you ten years before the Flood,
> And you should, if you please, refuse
> Till the conversion of the Jews.

In the same poem, he uses understatement to clinch his argument for seduction:

> The grave's a fine and private place,
> But none, I think, do there embrace.

Substitute "we know" for "I think," and the brilliant wit of the couplet would vanish.

PARADOX

Paradox is a figure of speech distinct from irony but not always easy to distinguish. It consists of an apparent contradiction that is nonetheless true and finally explicable, often for psychological reasons. Examples would be "Shyness is a form of vanity" (one thinks one is important enough to attract attention) and "Self-love is a prerequisite for loving others" (otherwise we are insecure and distrustful). Even more so than irony, paradox is intellectually gritty, forcing the reader to think. Writers of maxims like La Rochefoucauld ("It is far better to be de-

ceived by one's friends than to distrust them") and essay-
ists like William Hazlitt ("On the Disadvantages of Intellectual Superiority") are often paradoxical; in fact they
derive much of their interest from jogging the reader into
new insights. But poets also use paradoxes, from simply
presenting *oxymorons*, which are paradoxes formed by
juxtaposing two contradictory words (proud humility, el-
oquent silence), to making a paradox the theme of an entire poem.

Tone, irony, and paradox are perhaps the most abstruse
elements in poetry. They cause the reader to pay the
strictest attention not only to what is said but to how it
is said; and in the case of a paradox the reader must try
to decide whether it is true and, if so, to explain it. It all
adds up to the expenditure of goodly amounts of mental
energy, but in many ways these demands on the intellect
are, when met successfully, the most rewarding of the
elements in poetry.

7

Poetic Devices of Sound
(onomatopoeia, alliteration, assonance, consonance, repetition, cacophony and euphony)

Besides meanings, words have sounds that can be manipulated, and since poems are composed of words, sound can be an important element in a poem; it can itself convey meaning. But poetic sound devices are most often supportive of the sense of a poem rather than existing for their own sake. In any case, any time the sound of a poem appears unusual, whether, for example, it be in repetition or in difficulty of pronunciation, look for the source of the sound pattern and its function, if any.

ONOMATOPOEIA

When the sound of a word directly reflects its sense, it is *onomatopoeic: snap, crackle, pop, bow-wow.* Such words can add to the immediacy of a passage, but their use is obviously limited. Words like *rattle* or *bark*, which are only close in the relation of sound to meaning, may also provide life to a passage of verse, as they do in any context, but they are not, strictly speaking, onomatopoeic; it is better to say that the sound resembles the action, in those instances where it is worthwhile to point it out at all.

A whole passage may sometimes be said to be onomatopoeic where the sound reflects the content, but to say rather that the sound echoes the sense is preferable. This expression derives from Alexander Pope's comment on poetry in his *Essay on Criticism* (1711): "The sound must seem an Echo to the sense" (line 365). Pope goes on to give a tour de force of sound effects:

> Soft is the strain when Zephyr gently blows,
> And the smooth stream in smoother numbers flows;
> But when loud surges lash the sounding shore,
> The hoarse, rough verse should like the torrent roar:
> When Ajax strives some rock's vast weight to throw,
> The line too labours, and the words move slow;
> Not so when swift Camilla scours the plain,
> Flies o'er th' unbending corn, and skims along the main.

The meaning has something to do with causing the sound to convey an echo, for such passages have often been reprinted with only slightly different-sounding words, but with entirely different meaning, and consequent loss of the soft or harsh or laborious effects. The third and fourth lines above lose some of their loud roar when so revised:

> But when cloud verges flash astounding more
> The source, puff worse, would strike abhorrent, soar.

And yet with the original words intact the effects are clearly there.

A more subtle example of sound echoing sense occurs in the first section of "Dover Beach":

Listen! you hear the grating roar
Of pebbles which the waves draw back, and fling,
At their return, up the high strand,
Begin, and cease, and then again begin,
With tremulous cadence slow, and bring
The eternal note of sadness in.

Much of the sound effect comes from the metrical lay-out, especially the extra-heavy stresses on certain words ("back, and fling," "then again begin") which echo the crashing of the waves, and the caesuras in the third through fifth lines above, which echo the interludes when the waves subside. The sound of the final two lines also resembles the long wash of the wave on the sand before it begins to go out again.

Part of the effect of the last two lines is provided by their tempo or speed, which is produced in a number of ways. In the line "With tremulous cadence slow, and bring," for example, there are long vowels (cadence slow), many monosyllabic words, a prominent caesura, and a certain difficulty of pronunciation (especially "tremulous cadence"). All four of these devices are often used to slow a line down; their absence and the presence of sound repetition in a line (such as alliteration) will, on the other hand, cause a line to speed up. Notice in the example, furthermore, that the idea of slowness is present, even the word *slow* itself.

ALLITERATION

Prosodists have sometimes considered several devices along with rime, so close is their resemblance in various ways: alliteration, assonance, and consonance. Like rime, they involve repetition of sound; they normally are found in stressed syllables only; and they must occur either in the same or nearby lines to function properly.

Alliteration is the repetition of *initial* consonant sounds: tried and true, fit as a fiddle, tick tock. As with so many other terms, alliteration has been loosely applied—in this case, to initial consonant sounds that are not actually the same: steep strand, broken back. These sounds (*st* and *str, br* and *b*) are clearly not the same and should be designated as repetition of *st* sounds and *b* sounds rather than alliteration, because, for one thing, they are not nearly as effective.

Sound devices such as alliteration are only of interest, and should only be pointed out at all, if they function in their poetic context. For repetition of initial consonant sounds is common in English and indeed is not always avoidable.

One function of alliteration, in any event, is to link related words, as in cummings's "when faces called flowers": "but keeping is downward and doubting . . ." (line 3), "but keeping is doting and nothing and nonsense . . ." (line 10). The main effect for which alliteration is used, however, is to emphasize the words involved. In "Icy Harvest," for example, we are told that the hearts of the horses "had reached a *st*ony *st*op," and the alliterated words, in conjunction with the meter, emphasize that stop dramatically. In the same poem the emphasis of alliteration helps to make the sound of another passage echo the sense—"she *sk*immed a*wa*y on *ska*tes"—where the back-and-forth motion of skating is conveyed by the meter, alliteration, and by assonance.

ASSONANCE

In the last example, *assonance,* the repetition of similar vowel sounds, occurs in the long *a* sounds in "away" and "skates" and provides some of the swaying movement by bringing more stress to the syllables involved. In an earlier passage, a similar echoing movement is obtained by assonance: "And pushing heavy blocks that bobbed along" (line 3). Here the heavy short *o* sound in "blocks," "bobbed," and "along" combines with the regular meter to provide a resemblance to the ponderous motion of the ice blocks that "bobbed" (a word which, by its contrary connotations of quick up-and-down motion, helps further to convey the sluggish movement).

CONSONANCE

A repetition of similar consonant sounds before and after different vowels (like/look, lean/alone), *consonance* is more difficult to come by in English and less used in poetry. W. H. Auden, nevertheless, built an entire poem, "O Where are you going?" out of a pattern of consonance with combinations such as "reader/rider," "fearer/farer," "horror/hearer." Consonance, of course, attracts a great deal of attention to the words in which it occurs, and would consequently have to be used sparingly or as part of an obvious pattern, as in Auden's poem. Consonance is sometimes used to provide half-rime, as in lines 2 and 4 of "Grandparents": "spin"/"span."

REPETITION

Not often discussed in its own right, the simple *repetition* of whole words and phrases beyond the use of stanza repetition and refrains is an important sound device often used by poets. Its function is usually to provide rhetorical emphasis of an obvious kind; when a phrase is repeated its meaning tends to stand out. In "Dover Beach" we have an instance; the speaker claims that the modern world

> Hath really neither joy, nor love, nor light,
> Nor certitude, nor peace, nor help for pain. . . .

The pileup of the negatives, especially in conjunction with so many monosyllables, leaves the reader with a very heavy sense of emptiness: by the time you finish the list you realize the world is clearly an unhappy place in which to live.

But verbal repetition can also work in more imaginative ways. The fourth stanza in "Death in Leamington" is not intended to emphasize the initial repeated word:

> She bolted the big round window,
> She let the blinds unroll,
> She set a match to the mantle,
> She covered the fire with coal.

The purpose of the repetition here is rather to emphasize the similarity in sentence structure in each line, for the point of the stanza is to reflect the crisp, mechanical efficiency of the nurse in the crisp, mechanical efficiency of the syntax.

In the second lines of each stanza of cummings's "when faces called flowers," there is a good deal of repetition of an unusual sort. Each line provides its own equation:

> and breathing is wishing and wishing is having—
>
> and wishing is having and having is giving—
>
> and having is giving and giving is living—

$a = b$ and $b = c$ and so $a = c$. Not only is there the repetition of words in each line, but the second statement of each line is the same as the first of the next; consequently a long equation is set up. Breathing is wishing is having is giving is living. Thus we come full circle: breathing is living.

CACOPHONY AND EUPHONY

Respectively defined as the unpleasant and pleasant combination of sounds, *cacophony* and *euphony* function like other devices of sound in reflecting the sense of the passage in which they occur. That is, if a passage is unpleasant, the sounds of the words chosen are often unpleasant as well, and vice versa. At the height of the distasteful imagery in "Icy Harvest" we are presented with a profusion of difficult *t* and *s* sounds:

> Thick tongues protruded; icicles encroached. . . .

Following this somewhat tongue-twisting line, we are given a contrasting image of the previously pleasant condition of the same mouths conveyed by sounds equally pleasant:

> On mouths that often, warm and velvety. . . .

Smooth vowel sounds and few hard consonants are not accidental here. But sometimes cacophony *is* inadvertent and thus a flaw, as in line 23 of "Dover Beach":

> Lay like the folds of a bright girdle furled.

At least there is no apparent reason for the sound of the line to be so difficult to articulate.

Sounds in a poem can be manipulated for effect, modulated to convey subtle nuances of meaning. The effects are more obvious when the poems are read aloud, but even in a silent reading they are there leading your ear and your mind.

8

Evaluation
(relativism, sentimentality, cliché, formal criticism)

The ability to evaluate ourselves, others, and our environment has been proposed more than once as the whole object of a liberal arts education. Be that as it may, surely one of the main objects of a study of literature is to be able to tell the good from the not-so-good or bad.

And yet the ability to judge meaningfully, or in anything but a subjective way, has been called into question gradually for the past three hundred years or so until today most of us are hesitant to make evaluations of any kind. We are predisposed rather to ask whether we can judge a poem at all and what it means if we do. Isn't it all a matter of taste, whatever that means?

RELATIVISM

It is true that philosophical issues must be faced by those who wish to make objective judgments. Values, in order to be objective and unchanging, would have to exist outside nature, for change is a quality of natural things. *Critical relativism,* the concept that in fact all values are relative to the individual, that thus no value judgments can be anything more than private opinion, is one answer to the question and the one most likely to be encountered today.

Two subcategories of relativism are *historical relativism* and *cultural relativism.* The first view, which has been around longer, sees values as changing from age to age. Look, for example, it argues, at the variety of opinion about Shakespeare's works from the time they were written. When we judge a work we are clearly only doing so for our own age. Cultural relativism, a fairly recent view, argues that values belong to one's culture and differ from culture to culture with no possibility of judgment between any of them that wouldn't merely reflect the prejudices of the judge's own culture. We may believe Shakespeare a great writer, but a Fiji Islander may not, and who is to say who's right (whatever right means under the circumstances)? There is simply no platform outside of the variety of cultures from which to judge.

For even the values of an age or of a particular culture or (better yet) of a particular culture in a particular age can afford no real objectivity: the best such values can do is to appeal to a collective subjective, which is a mere matter of statistics, not finally very satisfying to someone concerned with judging the fundamental value of a work.

The ramifications of relativism are vast and to some minds unsettling. If relativism is true, it is impossible to set limits; *all* value judgments must be ultimately the result of subjective taste alone. All the poetry in this book was originally chosen by editors of magazines and publishing houses based on personal taste or cultural prepossessions and then chosen by the editor of this book on the same bases. Good, bad, or indifferent are terms utterly irrelevant in this view.

There is, however, a viable alternative. There has been, one might argue, a remarkable amount of agreement about Shakespeare from age to age—he has almost always been admired for the same basic reasons. And the differences in tastes among cultures can be explained by the level of cultural development involved (to avoid circular argument, a higher culture is defined as one in which human potential can be more fully realized). If the Fiji Islanders dislike Shakespeare, it is probably because they are not sufficiently advanced culturally to understand him. But their dislike is only hypothetical anyway; there is no reason to think that they would not appreciate a writer as universal in his interests as Shakespeare.

For there is a basic uniformity to human nature; all persons are *essentially* alike. There are some views and feelings that are culturally imposed, but all feel the same basic emotions—fear, envy, hate, delight, and so on. Traditional values and even enduring judgments, moreover, suggest a kind of permanence and objectivity in value judgments. How could literary works, like the epics of Homer and tragedies of Sophocles, have survived across temporal and cultural barriers if there is nothing objective involved?

If something develops from conscious choices, as does poetry, it is difficult to believe the choices cannot be judged meaningfully as good or bad choices, beyond merely subjective considerations. Earlier in this book a set of traditional beliefs about literature was set forth, and if we can agree about what literature is and what it does, then we can also discuss how literary ends are best accomplished. From basic premises about literature, more-specific principles can be derived and discussed, and if agreement ensues, objective evaluation becomes a distinct possibility.

No one, of course, can ever *wholly* rise above subjective prejudices in making judgments, but with this qualification in mind we can attempt humbly and flexibly to make judgments about literature that go beyond ourselves and our age. By doing so, we become involved in a worthwhile endeavor: to promote the good and discourage the not-so-good or downright bad. The philosophical problems of the position can even be ignored if necessary: we can say simply that objective values appear to exist although we don't know how. With a theistic point of view, there is no difficulty at all, for traditionally, absolute values have from the time of Plato been seen to exist in the One, or God.

Perhaps the most important point to remember in making judgments about literature is that they are all subject to human fallibility. But if you apply your reason and experience (of both life and literature) to a poem and bring to bear principles that are well thought out and reasonably sound, your judgments should themselves be sound and worthwhile. It is human to judge things (whether we like it or not), and it probably doesn't make a great deal of difference whether we believe our judgments are an attempt to evaluate fundamental qualities in a poem or are merely an expression of our subjective predilections—except in the amount of seriousness with which we do the job and value the judgment.

SENTIMENTALITY

If literature does indeed represent human experience and interpret it in the process, one of the largest literary problems for the last two hundred years or so has been sentimentality. Normally used as a negative term, *sentimentality* describes a condition in which more emotional response is forthcoming than a situation calls for naturally. There is considerable difference in weeping at the death of a friend and sobbing over a crushed grasshopper, although, under more complex conditions, such assessments are a bit more difficult to make.

Like most flaws in human nature, sentimentality has been used by lazy writers to avoid going to the trouble of appealing naturally to our feelings. By now, many subjects—mother love, first love, babies and small animals—have become easy conductors for a conditioned response. By treating such a subject in certain ways to elicit stock responses, the sentimental poet manages to ring an emotional bell, and like Pavlov's dog, we salivate. It is even possible that if we are not aware of this tampering with our emotions we can end up with no real sentiments at all—and worst of all, not even know it.

Sentimentality has been around a long time; the world seems to pass through cycles during which it is pervasive. After the height of the Hellenic period in Greece, during which Aeschylus and Sophocles wrote their great tragedies, came Euripides and the beginning of Hellenistic emotionalism. In his *Alcestis,* the heroine's young boy responds to his mother's passage to the Underworld:

> Father, I am too small to be left alone
> by the mother I loved so much. Oh,
> it is hard for me to bear
> all this that is happening,
> and you, little sister, suffer
> with me too. Oh, father,
> your marriage was empty, empty she did not live
> to grow old with you.

translated by Richmond Lattimore

One need not have spent much time around children to realize that they do not react this way nor do they have such loving relationships with their siblings. The emotions expressed are phony; the dramatic situation is milked for all it's worth. Aristotle, for whom Homer and Sophocles represented great writers, had a good deal less use for Euripides in the *Poetics*.

One of the tasks of literature, according to William Wordsworth, writing near the beginning of the present Romantic cycle (in his preface to *Lyrical Ballads* [1802]), is exactly to thwart sentimentality:

> For the human mind is capable of being excited without the application of gross and violent stimulants; and he must have a very faint perception of its beauty and dignity who does not know this, and who does not further know, that one being is elevated above another, in proportion as he possesses this capability. It has therefore appeared to me, that to endeavour to produce or enlarge this capability is one of the best services in which, at any period, a Writer can be engaged; but this service, excellent at all times, is especially so at the present day.

But the typical best-seller and the popular poetry of Anne Morrow Lindbergh and others have encouraged sentimentality, not curbed it.

The subjects used, however, are not intrinsically sentimental; it is rather the treatment of subjects that makes them so. Even so volatile a subject as the love of a boy for his grandfather can, if handled with care, evoke real sentiment, not sentimentality. In "Grandparents," Robert Lowell forces the emotion to a very high pitch:

> Never again
> to walk there, chalk our cues,
> insist on shooting for us both.
> Grandpa! Have me, hold me, cherish me!

But he does not milk the situation; rather he immediately undercuts the runaway emotion brilliantly with the next phrase: "Tears smut my fingers." "Smut" is exactly the word wanted, for with all its negative connotations it squelches sentimentality and brings the reader up short. Then follows the very touching scene of the speaker, almost a boy again in his anger at the past for being past, doing what he would have done as a boy to annoy his grandfather. It is altogether a tour de force of emotional control.

Sentimentality is normally seen as a surplus of emotion, a sentimentalist as a sensitive soul with emotions bubbling over. But sentimentality is perhaps really a cover-up for a lack of emotions. Most often if you scratch a sentimentalist you find a cynic, one who conceals a very dismal view of life. For such a one, the rose-colored lens of sentimentality is what makes it all bearable. One can, however, be a realist—even a skeptic—without being a cynic and sentimentalist. Life is not so bad that we must coat it with treacle.

CLICHÉ

Sentimentality sometimes finds its way into otherwise successful poems—for example, into this passage from Siegfried Sassoon's "The Child at the Window":

> The brave March day; and you, not four years old,
> Up in your nursery world—all heaven for me.
> Remember this—the happiness I hold—
> In far off springs I shall not live to see. . . .

The subject matter is hazardous to begin with, and the treatment is borderline sentimental at places ("all heaven for me")—the poet should have been more careful. But the use of trite expressions, or clichés, is encountered less frequently in the sorts of poems read in college, even though clichés share with sentimentality the use of conditioned responses. "With your head held high" in a patriotic poem or "With a heart so true" in a love poem are so many counters negotiable on the emotion exchange. The relative infrequency of such rhetorical flourishes in good poetry is no doubt owing to the skill with words possessed by good poets, who do share our problems dealing with emotions.

FORMAL CRITICISM

Most often, poetry worthy of the name suffers rather from flaws in technique in, for example, meter, diction, or imagery. For as anyone knows who has ever seriously attempted to write poetry, each poem presents certain peculiar problems in conveying what it is you wish to convey. Language often resists manipulation; images frequently just won't come; one has occasionally to settle for an unsatisfactory line of verse.

The poetry of Sir Walter Scott offers innumerable examples of formal flaws, for, although he was a competent and even inspired poet at points, he was often careless in his verse writing. In *Marmion,* a verse romance, occur the lines:

> The Monarch o'er the siren hung
> And beat the measure as she sung;
> And, pressing closer, and more near,
> He whispered praises in her ear.

The phrasing "closer, and more near" is redundant and is obviously present to pad out the line and provide a rime. Scott even indulged in a grammatical error in the same poem to get an easy rime: "Even such weak minister as me / May the oppressor bruise." ("Me," not "oppressor," is the subject of the sentence; "me" should, of course, read "I.")

But the most interesting flaw in the poem occurs in the battle scene:

> Then Eustace mounted too:—yet staid
> As loath to leave the helpless maid,
>> When, fast as shaft can fly,
> Bloodshot his eyes, his nostrils spread,
> The loose rein dangling from his head,
> Housing and saddle bloodyred,
>> Lord Marmion's steed rushed by. . . .

Such confusion of antecedents is hilarious but inexcusable, even in a long poem such as *Marmion.*

In short poems there are usually fewer formal errors, if for no other reason than that the poet has less to revise and polish, but even the short poems chosen for the brunt of the discussion in this text contain a few flaws. The last images in "when faces called flowers" seem to me confusing:

> all the pretty birds dive to the heart of the sky
> all the little fish climb through the mind of the sea. . . .

If the poet means to convey that all things are finally One, there are surely less-obscure ways of doing so. In the last chapter, furthermore, I remarked on the apparently inadvertent cacophony in a line in "Dover Beach." In Robert Lowell's "Grandparents" there are likewise several lines that seem accidentally out of harmony:

> I hear the rattley little country gramophone
> racking its five foot horn. . . .

You might make a case that the dissonance echoes the sense—the "rattley . . . gramophone"—but it seems more likely the result of poor word choice.

When flaws occur in a poem, they should be pointed out as part of the analysis; such flaws are significant properties of a poem. But several critical principles are

worth considering as well. If the flaw is fairly unimportant or defensible on some ground or other, it is perhaps
an opportunity to evoke "poetic license," which has been
defined as "what a poet can get away with." And, more
important, just as it is not profane to find a flaw in a poem
to begin with, so an occasional flaw doesn't ruin a poem—
there are usually compensations. Adverse criticism,
moreover, does not imply superiority; one should never
consider oneself in an adversary or competitive relationship to the poet. But it is the responsibility of the poet
and the reader to ask of poetry the best it has to give, and
that can only be accomplished through evaluation.

9

Explication of a Text
(how to write about a poem)

Explication of a poetic text
—the description and analysis of a poem—is to some extent a French invention of the late nineteenth century. *Explication de texte* involves a strict format that presents an extremely thorough reading of a poem or part of a poem. Every sound and every nuance of meaning are scrutinized, analyzed, and discussed at some length.

Explication as practiced in Britain and America is less structured and usually less thorough. There is in fact no set way of going about the job, although there are a few norms to guide one. Student papers explicating a poem of 10–30 lines tend to be short assignments, often running three to four pages (double-spaced). The reader of such a paper expects an overview of the poem, some data concerning its form, a statement of its meaning, an examination of any particularly difficult passages—all this topped off with a general comment on the poem or an evaluation of it.

Most often the central part of the paper deals with the poem more or less in the order it appears upon the page, from the beginning to the end. The structure or strategy of the poem—"here the poet is setting the scene or the mood" or "here he presents a section with a transitional idea"—usually provides the organization of the commentary. Within that organization the student discusses the work's poetic devices and how they support the strategy of the poet. There are other ways to proceed, but this progressive movement through the poem is usually the easiest and the clearest; it is certainly recommended for the beginner. The following suggested procedures, in any event, follow the above standards. Now that you have read chapters containing detailed discussions of poetic devices and techniques, it is time to pull all the material together and put it to use.

PRELIMINARY READING

1. Look for the meaning of the poem—what the poem is about, what the poet apparently intended. Watch out for any details that do not fit into your initial reading. Try to subsume them into a different reading until no inconsistencies or conflicts remain. What you are striving for is the most-likely reading.

2. Look for the overall structure of the poem. Try to determine the strategy the poet used to present the meaning, the theme. What *kind* of a poem is it—narrative, dramatic, satiric, reflective, lyric, or a combination of these? Often you must first determine who the speaker or speakers of the poem are and what the tone is.

3. Look for poetic devices for which terms exist (e.g., simile, alliteration), for they are usually the most im-

portant, and try to determine how they function. Especially watch out for subtle effects that you can explain as working through the use of devices or combinations of devices.

4. Look for words that are used in unusual ways or that are seemingly out of place, and try to decide their function, if any.

5. Look for lines or sections of the poem that require explanation and do your best to understand them.

ORGANIZATION OF THE MATERIAL

1. Begin with an introductory paragraph supplying the "vital statistics" of the poem—the author's name, the title, the kind or genre of poem, the versification, and the meaning. To learn terminology is usually one goal in taking an introductory course in poetry, and thus what may seem a merely mechanical procedure provides a useful function—the practical application of knowledge. This general description of the poem can and should be handled deftly; if you write it like a laundry list, it will sound like a laundry list.

2. In the body of the paper, follow the structure of the poem if it is distinct (stanzas, sections, logical divisions). Otherwise you may organize your discussion by groups or patterns of devices, such as imagery, but you should still do so in order of progression. If you don't, you tend to omit a lot of interesting material and risk losing the reader's comprehension. Often you can structure your discussion of the poem around the apparent strategy of the poet in dealing with the theme (for instance, setting the scene, presenting the first argument by anecdote). You should always try to show how the devices and diction fulfill the poet's needs in any given section of the poem.

Don't be afraid to present what seems to you an

interesting but possibly mistaken analysis of a device as long as you qualify your comments by admitting your awareness of that possibility. Often very sensitive and intelligent readings are abandoned from a false sense of a need for certainty.

3. At the end of your analysis you should comment on the poem. You can, for instance, evaluate the success of the poem, or discuss the ramifications of the theme, or point out some peculiarity in the poet's handling of devices. Whatever you do, you should stress the overall unity of the poem, for you have taken the poem apart, and it deserves to be treated as a whole again.

4. Try *not* to provide an unnecessary and boring paraphrase of the entire poem. You can assume that your reader has access to the poem itself and understands poetic terminology. You should also avoid pointing out the presence of poetic devices the function of which you are unable to discuss. There is nothing either pertinent or interesting about the mere presence of alliteration in a line.

5. If you find you haven't enough to say about the poem to fill the assigned number of pages, you most likely have not spent sufficient time analyzing the poem. The problem, especially in an assignment of three to four pages, should lie rather in eliminating discussion of less-important techniques; your handling of this challenge will in fact show that you can distinguish what is important.

The explication of a poem, like the serious reading of poetry itself, should not be seen as a chore or as a kind of make-work exercise. You are dealing with a poem—that is, with what is preeminently a work of art. Explication is likewise not merely a form of entertainment, like working a crossword puzzle, although there is surely a similar excitement involved in suddenly discovering the inner workings of a poem. But the depth of understanding that comes from the need to verbalize your analysis of a work of art goes beyond such intermediate pleasures. It should be one of the most intellectually and emotionally satisfying activities available to us, short of writing the poetry itself.

Appendix I
Explications

Dover Beach:
An Explication

Matthew Arnold's "Dover Beach" is a modern poem about a modern condition. We are given a dramatic situation with a speaker talking to his love inside a building on the English coast within view of the white cliffs of Dover and a lighthouse across the English Channel. He reflects on the condition of a world with Christianity dwindling away, leaving a purposeless universe devoid of the human values he cherishes. As might be expected, the tone of this dramatic-reflective poem is somber, the mood conveyed by an iambic meter with both irregular line lengths and irregular rime.

The first section sets the physical scene just described and is especially rich in sound effects. In lines 3 and 4 the sound seems to echo the sense in describing one of the images:

—ŏn thĕ / Frénch cóast / thĕ líght
Gleáms ănd / ĭs góne. . . .

The word "light," occurring as it does at the end of the line, receives a heavier-than-normal stress, and it is followed (over the line break) by the substitution of a trochee with a heavy first stress on "gleams," followed by two weak unstressed syllables ("and is") and then the stressed "gone." I submit that a beam from a lighthouse follows temporally the same pattern, with the beam visible as it swings through the sea mist, followed by sudden brightness as the light hits the viewer directly, and then dimming as the light sweeps away.

The tone suddenly becomes more ominous with the word "Only" in line 7, which takes a heavy stress on the first syllable both from the substitution of a trochaic for an iambic foot and from the long *o* sound. An impressive image follows in the next line: "moon-blanched land" conveys clearly the effect of moonlight on a landscape; the view is almost as distinct as in daylight with one exception—all the color is gone, blanched out.

With the direction "Listen" opening line 9, the imagery naturally changes to auditory; the sound of the rest of the first section in fact supports the sense as well:

> Listen! you hear the grating roar
> Of pebbles which the waves draw back, and fling,
> At their return, up the high strand,
> Begin, and cease, and then again begin,
> With tremulous cadence slow, and bring
> The eternal note of sadness in.

Much of the sound effect comes from the metrical layout, especially the extra-heavy stresses on certain words ("báck, aňd flíng," "thén ăgaín běgín") which echo the crashing of the waves, and the caesuras in lines 10 and 12, which echo the interludes when the waves subside. The sound of lines 12 and 13 also resembles the long wash of the wave on the sand before it begins to go out again, an effect partly provided by the slowing of the lines with many long vowels, monosyllabic words, and some difficulty in pronunciation (especially "tremulous cadence").

From an overview of the structure of the entire poem, the second section emerges as a transition between the somber sound of the waves in the first and the somber thoughts in the third. In a breathtaking maneuver it moves quickly from reality (the sea) to a metaphor (Sophocles) to the use of reality (the sea) as a new metaphor (the Sea of Faith).

The whole of the third section is in fact the "thought" mentioned in line 19. The speaker bemoans the recession of Christianity expressed here as "the Sea of Faith," which was at high tide during the Middle Ages and early Renaissance. The imagery that had become visual again reverts to auditory after line 24, with another slow line full of assonance and caesuras echoing the sense: "Its melancholy, // long, // withdrawing // roar." The final image of this section is dreary, with Christianity metaphorically at ebb tide and with no return of the cycle anticipated.

With the fourth and final section there is a dramatic break in the reflection, and the speaker makes an emotional appeal to his love. Then the full implications of the religious withdrawal are elaborated. The moonlit world of the first section, "which seems / To lie before us like a land of dreams" (lines 30–31), is not what it appears. With the repetition first of "so" in line 32 and then of "nor" in lines 33–34, there is a heavy stress placed on what is missing, with a consequent buildup of a tone of despair. Most of the missing qualities—"joy," "love," "light," "peace"—were perhaps especially chosen for their Christian associations: "I bring you tidings of great joy," "God is *love*," "I am the *light* of the world," "*Peace* I leave with you, my peace I give you." The final image of the night battle, being also a simile, does not necessarily refer to any particular war; it compares modern purposeless life to a battlefield at night with its senseless slaughter and utter confusion. The battlefield, furthermore, resembles the seascape before him in its unawareness or indifference, although this connection is not made overtly.

It is ironic (and pathetic) that the two qualities sought

by the speaker in his appeal in lines 29–30, love and faith-fulness or certitude, are precisely what he subsequently claims are now missing from the world; nor is there the peace or help for his pain that he so urgently seeks. What might seem, in any case, like escapism in his grasping at romantic straws does not really seem so on considera-tion. Involved in the modern condition, he has at least had the honesty to look straight at what so many people prefer to ignore, the spiritual consequences of their philo-sophic views. If reason has led him inexorably to despair and he turns to feeling as a last resort, it is perhaps be-cause he can find no alternative.

Grandparents: Much in Little

The emotion contained in Robert Lowell's very emo-tional poem "Grandparents" is carefully controlled by the complicated strategy of the poet. The volatile subject, the reflection of the speaker upon his childhood affection for his grandfather, is conveyed without a story or a dramatic situation, although the reflection does take place at a spe-cific location—the "farm" retreat near Brockton, Massa-chusetts, inherited by the speaker from his well-to-do grandparents. The free verse (which has, however, some rime and half-rime) is tightly controlled for emotional ef-fect.

The opening section, which introduces the grandpar-ents and their situation during the speaker's earlier visit as a young adolescent, is the easiest to follow but also the most rewarding for analysis of devices, especially diction. In the first line, we are told they are "altogether otherworldly now," the "altogether" tipping us off that the "otherworldly" is a pun, meaning both dead (in the "other" world) and outlandish, as we find the appearance of the couple described in similes in lines 5–8: a policeman with a nightstick and a Mohammedan in purdah. Like horses, moreover, they metaphorically "champ at the bit" to go shopping once a week.

The expression "those adults" (line 2) takes us back to the child's view at the earlier time. The speaker was then in his "throw-away and shaggy span of adolescence," that is, his early teens when he was quickly outgrowing his clothes and was unkempt in appearance.

The diction becomes still more packed with meaning in lines 7–8, where his grandmother's "lavender mourning and touring veil" tells us that she was of that sort of thrifty rich folk who get double duty from their possessions; in this case her veil is lavender, dark enough for a funeral, but unfunereal enough (unlike black) for automobile touring. But the most significant words in the first section are "Grandpa" in line 5 and "Grandmother" in line 7, for taken together they tell you that the speaker felt close to the first and not to the second.

We know from the grandparents' possession of a Pierce Arrow, an expensive car, that they are well off. The car metaphorically "clears its throat" or roars its engine (line 9) to complement its being kept (literally) in a horse stall at a time before garages were common. The car then moves off, whitening the leaves, already "fatigued" by the summer heat, and taking with it the grandparents and by association "the nineteenth century" as well, to which they so clearly belong. They belong to a century that believed that "children should be seen and not heard," an allusion somewhere in the background of the phrase "tired of children" (line 12). That the car moves off into the sunlight may also be behind the direct literary allusion in the next line—"They're all gone into a world of light"—an almost verbatim rendition of the first line of a poem by Henry Vaughn, a seventeenth-century English poet and mystic. Since Vaughn's poem is a meditation on immortality, the allusion deepens the meaning of Lowell's line, taking it beyond the mere meaning that the grandparents are in the "other" world.

The first line of the second section ("The farm's my own!") picks up the last phrase of the previous line, thereby emphasizing it—the sound is so strong that it perhaps is meant to convey the slamming of a door. For the second section has the speaker inside the farmhouse and moving about, "spoil[ing] another season," as his grandmother might have put it. He moves past a gramophone—in a line that may either be inadvertently cacophonous or intended to echo the sense:

> I hear the rattley little country gramophone. . . .

Then, in the billiards room, the speaker in a metaphor compares the hanging lights over the table to spiders dangling on their threads, ironically, for the grandparents are the *ancien regime*, or the "Old Order," trying to keep "nature at a distance," and here nature figuratively intrudes. Nature appears again in the simile that follows: "No field is greener than its cloth" (line 23).

The reminiscences now become more specific, from the green tabletop, where his grandfather spilled coffee while dipping sugar cubes for them to eat, to the number three ball, to the stain underneath. The need to hide the stain of course tells us what sort of relationship existed between the grandparents and reinforces as well our knowledge of the ties between the grandfather and the boy, privy to his secret crime.

The reminiscence has become so intense that the last

section begins with an emotional cry from the speaker (lines 28–30):

> Never again
> to walk there, chalk our cues,
> insist on shooting for us both.

There is a heavy emphasis on the two words isolated in line 28 and the finality they convey through their sense; in line 29 there is internal rime ("walk"/"chalk"), which by likewise stressing these words conveys a kind of hurt disbelief. That the grandfather childishly insists on "shooting for us both" adds to the intensity of reminiscence that leads to the surprisingly emotional:

> Grandpa! Have me, hold me, cherish me!

In the Christian wedding service occur the words "to have," "to hold," and "to cherish" as descriptive of the relationship between husband and wife. Its echo here suggests the depth of the speaker's affection for his grandfather.

The poem at this point teeters on the brink of sentimentality. But in a move demonstrating extraordinary emotional control, Lowell undercuts any emotionalism: "Tears smut my fingers." "Smut" is precisely the word wanted, for with all its negative connotations, it brings the reader up short. Comic relief follows as the speaker, almost a boy again in his anger at the past for being past, does what he would have done as a boy to annoy his grandfather—draws mustaches on the Czar's picture. The grandfather would surely have resented such Bolshevik behavior.

So much is accomplished in the thirty-seven lines of this poem that one can only be awed. By an astonishingly economic use of diction and by tightly controlled strategy, Lowell accomplishes in a short poem what it might take a prose writer pages to match.

Death in Leamington: A Question of Tone

The point of John Betjeman's "Death in Leamington" is not easy to catch in the first several readings, for much of the meaning turns upon the tone, and the tone is complicated. It becomes clear after a while, however, that the poem is serious, that in fact it is a satire on the nurse who cares for the old woman, despite the lighthearted, whimsical feel of the versification. The bouncy iambic-anapestic meter and the ballad rime scheme (a b c b) contrast with the sense. There is even a breezy, balladlike elision in the word "ev'ning," which presumably was meant to work visually since the word would have been pronounced the same regardless of spelling. But the contrast of the poem's sound and sense paradoxically ends up reinforcing the sense.

There is almost no action in the poem; what there is takes place in a matter of minutes. The opening stanza sets the scene of the death: the "ev'ning star" tells us it is early evening, and we are told directly that the old woman is in an "upstairs bedroom." The detail of the "plate glass window" is probably intended to suggest that she is rich enough to afford plate glass. That Leamington is a "Spa," moreover, implies that the old woman has been living there for her health.

The second stanza continues with what amounts to an oblique metaphor:

> Beside her the lonely crochet
> Lay patiently and unstirred. . . .

The unusual modifiers "patiently and unstirred" suggest that the crochet is being subtly compared to a lapdog, the sort that is kept by old women. As a lifeless object identified with a live one, the crochet is thus placed in contrast to the nurse, who is alive but really "dead." This idea is continued in the next two lines, which present a simile comparing the fingers of the dead woman with "the spoken word," preparing us for the "dead" words of the nurse coming up in stanza five.

The nurse herself arrives in stanza three, "Breast high 'mid the stands and chairs," a description that suggests a rather buxom woman, crisp and straight-spined. But then we are informed that she

> was alone with her own little soul,
> And the things were alone with theirs.

The childish language, reinforced by the internal rime ("alone"/"own") and the simple repetition of "alone," anticipates the patronizing language of the nurse in stanza five and further suggests, by the implied comparison of her soul with that of "the things," that both are similarly endowed.

Stanza four has syntax as methodical and economic as the nurse. The "she" at the beginning of each line emphasizes the methodical side, as does the profusion of alliteration in the stanza: "bolted"/"big," "match"/"mantle," "covered"/"coal." The clear but monotonous sentence structures in any case carry us quickly to stanza five, where the alliteration and long vowels of "Tea" and "tiny" emphasize these words and consequently the obnoxiously patronizing tone of the nurse.

Then, in the middle of stanza five and continuing through the next stanza, we have an intrusion by the narrator, who is apparently so distressed by the nurse's speech that he addresses her directly. First he comments on her gaudy ("chintzy") cheeriness, and then he bombards her with a series of questions:

> Do you know that the stucco is peeling?
> Do you know that the heart will stop?
> From those yellow Italianate arches
> Do you hear the plaster drop?

He asks, in other words, whether she is aware of the inevitability of change and deterioration and death, thus countering her silliness and indifference with his own seriousness and concern. The presence of "Italianate arches" in a climate such as England's further implies a kind of phoniness about the situation.

During the second-to-last stanza, the nurse discovers her mistake; she scrutinizes "the gray, decaying face." The assonance emphasizes the words; the long vowels slow down the line; and the word "decaying" reminds us too that the woman is dead and what that means. But the seriousness evoked by these devices is offset in the next two lines by a tone that is both peaceful and mocking:

> As the calm of a Leamington ev'ning
> Drifted into the place.

You can almost visualize the nurse staring at the corpse during these two lines, for she moves swiftly in the last stanza once she's aware of death, and we once again witness her efficiency. The now unnecessary medicine bottles are moved aside. She tiptoes out from both habit and the similarity of death to sleep (noticeable by the whispers of people at funeral parlors). The illumination from the gaslight will no longer be needed; no sense wasting it.

It is clearly the nurse being satirized in "Death in Leamington," but the satire of her mechanical, unfeeling, and dishonest relationship with her patient probably is intended to be more universal than that. For it is easy for doctors and nurses and others caring for the sick to protect themselves after a while from the stress of witnessing pain and loneliness by withdrawing sympathy altogether. It is Betjeman's point, I believe, that should they do so, they are losers as well as their patients. There is perhaps more than one "death" in the room in Leamington.

when faces called flowers:
To Revive a Genre

Poems celebrating spring are at least as old as poetry; the problem of composing one today, however, is not so much a matter of originality—considering the subject, such poems could never have had much originality about them—but rather of conveying the excitement and wonder of the season, no matter how many one has seen come and go and no matter how many times the event has been celebrated in verse.

"when faces called flowers" by e. e. cummings succeeds where others have failed. The lyric simplicity of his poem is somewhat obscured by a very complicated stanza structure, but it all works to one end, excitement. The iambic-anapestic meter, for one thing, is appropriate in its bouncy enthusiasm. The rime scheme, moreover, is unobtrusive in that it exists only between stanzas (the first, fifth, and sixth lines of each), except in several instances of internal rime which occur in the same place in the fifth line of the first two stanzas ("spry"/"fly," "she"/"he"). And the repetition of words tends to maintain by emphasis the emotional heights reached earlier, repetition both between stanzas ("when" and "but keeping is," which open lines one and three of all three stanzas) and especially within stanzas (at the beginning of the last three lines of each: "yes," "now," "all," respectively).

The second lines of each stanza possess a kind of sense of their own when put together. Each line provides its own equation:

> and breathing is wishing and wishing is having—

> and wishing is having and having is giving—

> and having is giving and giving is living—

$a = b$, and $b = c$, and so $a = c$. The second statement of each line is the same as the first of the next; consequently a long equation is set up. Breathing is wishing is having is giving is living. Thus we come full circle: breathing is living.

The third lines of each stanza are likewise similar, each presenting a statement in contrast to the equations given above. The phrase "But keeping is" is repeated, and many parts of speech are interchanged, with adverbs and nouns performing the function of adjectives by tapping their negative connotations (emphasized by alliteration in several places): "downward," "never," "nothing," "nonsense," and so on.

The emotional peak of each stanza occurs in the fourth line. Each of these three lines contains the repetition of a word that helps the excitement along—"april(yes april; my darling)"—and each has a spontaneous address to the lover (the last stanza has merely the exclamation "O!").

Additional intensity is provided by a parenthetical comment as if the speaker is so caught up by his feelings he can't order his thoughts in a normal, straightforward manner but must interrupt himself.

Unexpected diction characterizes the fifth and sixth lines of each stanza, which refer to birds and fish respectively. The birds do not frolic as high as they can fly but "as spry as can fly," and fish, not lambs, "gambol." The suggestion of sex is, likewise, surprisingly conveyed by two words in stanza two that don't usually have erotic connotations, "hover" and "quiver." The "so she and so he" means "sexually," and the "so you and so I" in a parallel position link in the next line the speaker and his love with that idea. The diving of the birds "to the heart of the sky," however, and the climbing of the fish "through the mind of the sea" are perhaps too unusual; even if cummings is trying to convey that all nature is ultimately One, I find the sense of the images confusing.

The last line in each stanza, although somewhat different in collocation of words, acts as a kind of refrain. Each contains a biblical allusion: the image of a mountain dancing occurs in the 114th Psalm, and the allusion transforms what might sound silly into something joyful.

The imagery in cummings's poem, like the diction, is apparently designed to resemble as little as possible the shopworn verse of the past. The first line of the first stanza relies initially on the similarity of some flowers (like daisies) to faces and then moves off to evoke (at least for me) the image of time-lapse photography, which tends to give a floating, though jerky, effect of flowers growing and which thus would complement the animated-cartoon image of flowers with faces.

The first line of the middle stanza contains another impressive image:

when every leaf opens without any sound. . . .

The absence of sound implies a lack of fanfare, emphasizing the naturalness of the event, while the opening of *every* leaf suggests that it is happening all around and that one could not possibly keep track of them all in this outburst of spring. The first line of the final stanza contains no image, but the repetition of "has been found" conveys the excitement of recovery in spring of what was lost in winter.

cummings's poetry is known for disjointed syntax and dislocated parts of speech, but in no other of his poems are they perhaps so useful. For these peculiarities allow him to be different in a well-worn genre, and along with very imaginative imagery they provide him with the kind of excitement necessary to make a poem about spring a success.

Icy Harvest:
The Grim Reaper

Celeste Wright's "Icy Harvest," a poem about beauty and death and growing up, is for the most part given in narrative. Through the first two verse paragraphs we are told of several events in the winter day of a small girl, but the last short section leaves off the story and reflects upon the psychological effects of the events on the child. The poem is written in blank verse, which in its flow and unobtrusiveness is especially appropriate for narrative.

The first paragraph provides a view of the beautiful side of nature experienced by the girl. Men are cutting ice into blocks and storing them in an icehouse for use in a lakeside resort hotel somewhere up north, probably in New England. In line three the activity is reflected in the sound:

Aňd púshiňg héavỹ blócks thǎt bóbbed ǎlóng.   .   .

The assonance in "blocks," "bobbed," and "along" combines with the regular meter to provide a resemblance to the ponderous motion of the ice blocks that "bobbed," a word which, by its contrary connotations of quick up-and-down motion, helps further to convey the sluggish movement.

An extended metaphor generated by the title follows in lines 1 and 4 in the words "storehouse," "ice-crop," "garnered," "mealed." Then the diction becomes more suggestive. The reference to "the great hotel" in line 5 more than likely conveys the awed attitude of the natives toward the resort; it is perhaps even the expression used by them. The phrase "Old Amos" (line 6) suggests age and experience as well as the locale, for Old Testament names are more common in New England than elsewhere in the North. The playful alliteration of "pointed pole" sets the mood of the two of them as she "works" along with him as children will do. The last line of the section has a separate feeling about it; it sums up the tranquility of the scene:

The sunshine twinkled on the floating ice.

The presence of "twinkled" provides a hint of what's to come; it denotes the exact kind of motion of light on ice that is seen when it is beginning to melt. And of course it is the sun that is melting it.

The phrase "But later" rings in a change of mood at the beginning of the second verse paragraph, which indeed presents the other side of nature, the cruel and the ugly. The child "*sk*immed a*way* on *ska*tes" (line 9), with the back-and-forth movement of skating reflected in the heavy stresses provided by the alliteration, meter, and assonance. She then finds a crowd of lumberjacks near a hole in the ice, like mourners 'round a grave. Two dredge horses had drowned, and the diction becomes more intense to describe the event. The verb tense changes briefly from the past perfect ("had drowned") to the present participle "plunging" (line 12), more vividly to convey the action of the horses. Then their hearts "reached a *st*ony *st*op," with the alliteration and the meter combining to make the stop more emphatic. "Stony" also conveys the stone-deadness of the horses, perhaps even their frozen condition.

Our belief in the girl's reaction depends to some extent on how grimly the scene is presented, and so ghastly images continue almost to the end of section two, reinforced by deft use of poetic devices. A heavy effect is obtained by the assonance in line 15: "The b*o*dies, s*o*dden from the w*a*ter. . . ." A pun follows in line 17 ("With desperation frozen in their eyes"); both senses of *frozen*—"fixed" and "turned to ice"—are used, and in the process the appalling image of the wide, staring eyes is magnified. Distaste is augmented by the cacophony in line 18, with its profusion of difficult *t* and *s* sounds:

> Thick tongues protruded, icicles encroached. . . .

Then in the last two lines of the second section the mood changes to provide a contrast between the horror of the present scene and the beauty of her past friendship with the horses. Cacophony is replaced with euphony in line 19:

> On mouths that often, warm and velvety. . . .

The tactile imagery is especially pleasant here, as it is in the following line, where "lipped," rather than "licked," is more precisely descriptive of how horses would eat sugar from a palm.

The final paragraph describes the psychological effect of the gruesome scene of the dead horses. It begins with a personification ("Delight was murdered") which is a forceful and economic way of generalizing about that effect. The "glassy miles" in the same line goes beyond the more obvious metaphorical analogies of glass and ice—that both are hard, translucent, opaque, and shiny—to point up the fragile and alien nature of the girl's new world. "Terror now gaped" for her, we are told, just as the hole in the ice gaped, or the mouths of the horses. Finally, in a line deliberately parallel to line 8 with its twinkling sunshine, we have in the last line "the deceitful glitter of the sun," with the ambiguity of nature's role now clarified. "Glitter" may also be an allusion to "all that glitters is not gold" (a saying taken from a line in Shakespeare's *Merchant of Venice*, II, vii, 65); at least the point of the allusion, if it exists, matches the sentiment of the last line and of the poem as a whole.

Everyone, whether conscious of them or not, has experienced shocks in the process of growing up. Here the process is simply and clearly rendered in a three-part structure. The reaction of the young girl in the poem may appear extreme, but then the event portrayed is more violent than most, and she is after all a young child. She has confronted the ambivalence of nature and life, their beauty and their ugliness, a contrast also present in the title "Icy Harvest," ice representing cold and death, harvest signifying warmth and fruition. So too she has had from the experience a harvest of knowledge, unwelcome knowledge, an "Icy Harvest."

Appendix II
Some Additional Poems
Suitable for Analysis

Menelaus and Helen

I

Hot through Troy's ruin Menelaus broke
    To Priam's palace, sword in hand, to sate
    On that adulterous whore a ten years' hate
And a king's honour. Through red death, and smoke,
And cries, and then by quieter ways he strode,   5
    Till the still innermost chamber fronted him.
    He swung his sword, and crashed into the dim
Luxurious bower, flaming like a god.

High sat white Helen, lonely and serene.
    He had not remembered that she was so fair,   10
And that her neck curved down in such a way;
And he felt tired. He flung the sword away,
    And kissed her feet, and knelt before her there,
The perfect Knight before the perfect Queen.

II

So far the poet. How should he behold   15
    That journey home, the long connubial years?
    He does not tell you how white Helen bears
Child on legitimate child, becomes a scold,
Haggard with virtue. Menelaus bold
    Waxed garrulous, and sacked a hundred Troys   20
    'Twixt noon and supper. And her golden voice
Got shrill as he grew deafer. And both were old.

Often he wonders why on earth he went
    Troyward, or why poor Paris ever came.

Oft she weeps, gummy-eyed and impotent;   25
    Her dry shanks twitch at Paris' mumbled name.
So Menelaus nagged; and Helen cried;
And Paris slept on by Scamander side.

Rupert Brooke (1887–1915)

The Bottom Line

Love isn't a poem in the head
no matter what you think. It's
a hard grab from below that
tells you now, now,
& will stand no refusal.   5

Whatever name we give it
doesn't matter. The chicken
knows this, swooning with her mate
she makes no pact but the meeting,
feathers spread stiff,   10

& the dazzled rat that leaps through
our gutter is chasing a bald tail of love
So crazed by its smell he won't
see the cat, alive only
for a quick climb & shudder of fur.   15

The brown bear understands why
more than we can. He never falls
away, tricked by his mind into
weakness. Never wonders if he should
but hurries to couple, wet nose flared.   20

Listen, even the ones we
call cold-blooded do it better
Snakes & lizards come smooth,
blind with the weight of themselves
scales rub, glad for a chance,   25

& we rub, hiding
in some strange bed. Afraid
of this need that grips us—
out of words, naked, kneeling,
we fall in love again.   30

                              Mary Dougherty (1949–   )

Love's Noon

The sun has made it daylight everywhere,
Has melted the accustomed black of night
Into bright pools, where steeps my present care,
Until it too is fading into light.
Now look! The sun is climbing in the sky;   5
Last specks of darkness flare and disappear;
Before me blazing, joyous vistas lie:
I cast no shadow sunward through the years.
It should suffice, this present, future joy.
Why should I care what shadows fall behind?   10
But Love's proud sun will suffer no alloy
To his gold splendor; now sun-drenched I find
Him poised above, inviting mind to roam,
Past ransomed hours, the lonely streets back home.

John Ellsworth (1932–   )

Song

A rose, beguiled by early spring,
A flame so delicate,
The first chill damp, dispiriting,
Soon blasted, smothered it.

Our love was such a forward thing,   5
Too quick to shine, unfold;
It now lies smudged and withering.
Dear God! It is so dark, so cold.

John Ellsworth (1932–   )

Gang Rape

The afternoon shines hot on the thick
green water where she floats; where she fluffs
with lazy nods the feathers
of her second spring; where she bobs
then gobbles down the minnows flashing past   5
her gently paddling feet.

Then from the bank the slap of wings on water.
Through the tule and the cat-tail, jutting
in their season's flesh, rush five mallards,
enfrenzied with the blood of spring.   10

They sweep upon her, water boiling
as she sinks beneath their leader's weight.
His green skull-feathers glisten.
He raises bill toward heaven and splits the air
in harsh cacophony.   15

They follow one by one; each clenching at her ragged
neck. The waiting and the sated form a ring
of flailing wings as if to cloak their ravage.
And she, struggling beneath each courtier,
eyes bulging underwater as she squirms   20
to suck a lungful of that sweet spring air
sees nothing but the stifling green.

A stillness hovers once again above the lake.
The season's suitors have flown on
and afternoon is shining hot upon   25
the water where she floats;
her orange legs stiffening toward the angry sun.

Steve Ellzey (1954–   )   _____

For the Blue-Eyed Smiler on the Bus

I'd love to kiss you but your mother
would shriek; have me
thrown from the bus. So I wink;
grin back at you.
Then a tiny white fist   5
pushes out from your winter-bundled body;
fingers blossom as you reach
for my beard.

Slap   Mother wilts the flower.
"Don't touch the man."   10
She advises you with the tenderness
of a butcher's widow.
I must grin while you wail rebuked.
I must grin for the day when we slip
from this bus and leave mother screaming   15
behind tinted glass.

Steve Ellzey (1954–   )

Basey's Bike

Basey's bike
had the two of spades
clothespinned
to sputter in the spokes.
Basey knew   5
even before I broke his arm
that I was in his power.
My bike had fenders
and a chain guard
and a basket   10
and a buddy-seat in back.
Basey's bike was stripped for speed
and he rode like hell
with his pants leg rolled
and his threadbare crotch   15
buffing the bike frame to the iron.
Basey rode like a beating heart.

Even before I offered him
my plastic Indians
Basey knew I wanted to trade.   20
My paltry boot
(my 50 braves with savage names)
left him trading slightly down
but Basey took my mannered bike
and I possessed his wild machine   25
that seatless steed
that rush of painted metal.

Even before I broke his arm
Basey knew

he had me in his power.   30
Basey knew that I would quail
to see the front wheel wobble.
Basey knew that I would shrink
from awesome speed
with brakes that sometimes held   35
slipping in my mind.
I lamely begged an Indian trade.

Basey's arm broke when he fell.
I cried
to see him powerless.   40
I cried to see him
whimpering
atop his crooked arm
where I had thrown him.
Basey was small and frail   45
and broken beneath me
and his bike was bent
and shabby.
Basey knew as they picked him up
that I was in his power: 50
that twisted mouth
that beating heart
that skinny, wretched arm
crimped like the two of spades.

Kenneth Jones (1950–   )

Spider Killing

With two too many legs
and a gossamer treachery that stopped flies
and bound them in their own terror, spiders,
when I was younger, were to be killed.
The logic was unspoken, but I faithfully assumed   5
that insects were bugs; spiders, evil.

Wound a daddy-long-legs anywhere
and it would fall into a little pile
like so many broken brown threads;
the guts of a wolf spider stuck with a stick   10
oozed out creamy white like the center of a chocolate.

But now, on a Wednesday of nuclear-weapon tests,
nothing seems so uncertain as spider killing:
while technicians subvert the arid, flat face
of Nevada, testing gadgets that melt planets in theory,   15
incinerate revenue in practice, I stand
in my steamy bathroom and debate with myself
the death of a spider poised on the perspiring
ceramic tile.

I spare him, this time; then step   20
into the blasting shower and clouds of steam
pouring forth like fallout. The spider and I
stay in our steamed, vague corners
while Nevada's strata rumble
with the secrets of modern warfare.   25

The shadow of the Final War is a delicate cruelty,
strung across doorways and other passages,
sometimes stopping the mind and binding it
in a moment of terror.

Hans Ostrom (1954–   )

Calm and Fear

Juncos flit on snow,
then scatter like drops of water
on a griddle. What frightened them?
The awesome winter calm, perhaps;
or they had simply gone too long unafraid.   5

I want to comment on their sudden fear
or search an old bookcase
for a volume on birds. But instead I stand
silently at the window, the whiteness
where the birds were demanding vigilance.   10

I've been fishing, wading in the shadows, when a trout
spooks, rips a shred of shade
for its back and bullets over sunlit gravel.
I'm faintly glad that it frightens me
and for its fright.   15

A butterfly will sometimes drowse
in flight like a floating leaf,
then remember its body
like a startled, napping drunk and clap
its stiff wings, surprising itself aloft.   20

Often I'm afraid when I first
touch her; her gift of being here
and opening her arms
is awesome in the dark
after the accidental day.   25

Hans Ostrom (1954–   )

Proud Maisie

Proud Maisie is in the wood,
    Walking so early;
Sweet Robin sits on the bush,
    Singing so rarely.

"Tell me, thou bonny bird,   5
    When shall I marry me?"
"When six braw gentlemen
    Kirkward shall carry ye."

"Who makes the bridal bed,
    Birdie, say truly?"   10
"The grey-headed sexton
    That delves the grave duly.

"The glow-worm o'er grave and stone
    Shall light thee steady.
The owl from the steeple sing,   15
    'Welcome, proud lady.' "

Sir Walter Scott (1771–1832)

The Complaints of the Poor

And wherefore do the Poor complain?
    The Rich Man ask'd of me; . . .
Come walk abroad with me, I said,
    And I will answer thee.

'Twas evening, and the frozen streets   5
    Were cheerless to behold,
And we were wrapt and coated well,
    And yet we were a-cold.

We met an old bare-headed man,
    His locks were thin and white;   10
I ask'd him what he did abroad
    In that cold winter's night;

The cold was keen indeed, he said,
    But at home no fire had he,
And therefore he had come abroad   15
    To ask for charity.

We met a young bare-footed child,
    And she begg'd loud and bold;
I ask'd her what she did abroad
    When the wind it blew so cold;   20

She said her father was at home,
    And he lay sick a-bed,
And therefore was it she was sent
    Abroad to beg for bread.

We saw a woman sitting down
    Upon a stone to rest,
She had a baby at her back
    And another at her breast;   25

I ask'd her why she loiter'd there
    When the night-wind was so chill;   30
She turn'd her head and bade the child
    That scream'd behind, be still;

Then told us that her husband served,
    A soldier, far away,
And therefore to her parish she   35
    Was begging back her way.

We met a girl, her dress was loose
    And sunken was her eye,
Who with a wanton's hollow voice
    Address'd the passers-by;   40

I ask'd her what there was in guilt
    That could her heart allure
To shame, disease, and late remorse;
    She answer'd she was poor.

I turn'd me to the Rich Man then,   45
    For silently stood he, . . .
You ask'd me why the Poor complain,
    And these have answer'd thee!

Robert Southey (1774–1843)

To a Painter Attempting Delia's Portrait

Rash Painter! canst thou give the orb of day
In all its noontide glory? or pourtray
The diamond, that athwart the taper'd hall
Flings the rich flashes of its dazzling light?
Even if thine art could boast such magic might,   5
Yet if it strove to paint my angel's eye,
Here it perforce must fail. Cease! lest I call
Heaven's vengeance on thy sin: Must thou be told
The crime it is to paint divinity?
Rash painter! should the world her charms behold,   10
Dim and defiled, as there they needs must be,
They to their old idolatry would fall,
And bend before her form the pagan knee,
Fairer than Venus, daughter of the sea.

Robert Southey (1774–1843)

An Interlude

In the greenest growth of the Maytime,
    I rode where the woods were wet,
Between the dawn and the daytime;
    The spring was glad that we met.

There was something the season wanted,   5
    Though the ways and the woods smelt sweet;
The breath at your lips that panted,
    The pulse of the grass at your feet.

You came, and the sun came after,
    And the green grew golden above;   10
And the flag flowers lightened with laughter,
    And the meadowsweet shook with love.

Your feet in the full-grown grasses
    Moved soft as a weak wind blows;
You passed me as April passes,   15
    With face made out of a rose.

By the stream where the stems were slender,
    Your bright foot paused at the sedge;
It might be to watch the tender
    Light leaves in the springtime hedge,   20

On boughs that the sweet month blanches
    With flowery frost of May:
It might be a bird in the branches,
    It might be a thorn in the way.

I waited to watch you linger
  With foot drawn back from the dew,
Till a sunbeam straight like a finger
  Struck sharp through the leaves at you.

And a bird overhead sang *Follow*,
  And a bird to the right sang *Here*;   30
And the arch of the leaves was hollow,
  And the meaning of May was clear.

I saw where the sun's hand pointed,
  I knew what the bird's note said;
By the dawn and the dewfall anointed,   35
  You were queen by the gold on your head.

As the glimpse of a burnt-out ember
  Recalls a regret of the sun,
I remember, forget, and remember
  What Love saw done and undone.   40

I remember the way we parted,
  The day and the way we met;
You hoped we were both brokenhearted,
  And knew we should both forget.

And May with her world in flower   45
  Seemed still to murmur and smile
As you murmured and smiled for an hour;
  I saw you turn at the stile.

A hand like a white wood-blossom
  You lifted, and waved, and passed   50
With head hung down to the bosom,
  And pale, as it seemed, at last.

And the best and worst of this is
That neither is most to blame
If you've forgotten my kisses   55
And I've forgotten your name.

Algernon Charles Swinburne (1839–1909)

Old Man

Old Man, or Lad's-love—in the name there's nothing
To one that knows not Lad's-love, or Old Man,
The hoar-green feathery herb, almost a tree,
Growing with rosemary and lavender.
Even to one that knows it well, the names   5
Half decorate, half perplex, the thing it is:
At least, what that is clings not to the names
In spite of time. And yet I like the names.

The herb itself I like not, but for certain
I love it, as some day the child will love it   10
Who plucks a feather from the door-side bush
Whenever she goes in or out of the house.
Often she waits there, snipping the tips and shrivelling
The shreds at last on to the path, perhaps
Thinking, perhaps of nothing, till she sniffs   15
Her fingers and runs off. The bush is still
But half as tall as she, though it is as old;
So well she clips it. Not a word she says;
And I can only wonder how much hereafter
She will remember, with that bitter scent,   20
Of garden rows, and ancient damson trees
Topping a hedge, a bent path to a door,
A low thick bush beside the door, and me
Forbidding her to pick.

              As for myself,   25
Where first I met the bitter scent is lost.
I, too, often shrivel the grey shreds,
Sniff them and think and sniff again and try
Once more to think what it is I am remembering,

Always in vain. I cannot like the scent,   30
Yet I would rather give up others more sweet,
With no meaning, than this bitter one.

I have mislaid the key. I sniff the spray
And think of nothing; I see and I hear nothing;
Yet seem, too, to be listening, lying in wait   35
For what I should, yet never can, remember;
No garden appears, no path, no hoar-green bush
Of Lad's-love, or Old Man, no child beside,
Neither father nor mother, nor any playmate;
Only an avenue, dark, nameless, without end.   40

Edward Thomas (1878–1917)

Strange Fits of Passion Have I Known

Strange fits of passion have I known
And I will dare to tell,
But in the Lover's ear alone,
What once to me befell.

When she I loved looked every day   5
Fresh as a rose in June,
I to her cottage bent my way,
Beneath an evening moon.

Upon the moon I fixed my eye,
All over the wide lea;   10
With quickening pace my horse drew nigh
Those paths so dear to me.

And now we reached the orchard-plot;
And, as we climbed the hill,
The sinking moon to Lucy's cot   15
Came near, and nearer still.

In one of those sweet dreams I slept,
Kind Nature's gentlest boon!
And all the while my eyes I kept
On the descending Moon.   20

My horse moved on; hoof after hoof
He raised, and never stopped:
When down behind the cottage roof,
At once, the bright moon dropped.

What fond and wayward thoughts will slide   25
Into a Lover's head!
'O mercy!' to myself I cried,
'If Lucy should be dead!'

William Wordsworth (1770–1850)

The Old Cumberland Beggar

I saw an aged Beggar in my walk;
And he was seated, by the highway side,
On a low structure of rude masonry
Built at the foot of a huge hill, that they
Who lead their horses down the steep rough road   5
May thence remount at ease. The aged Man
Had placed his staff across the broad smooth stone
That overlays the pile; and, from a bag
All white with flour, the dole of village dames,
He drew his scraps and fragments, one by one;   10
And scanned them with a fixed and serious look
Of idle computation. In the sun,
Upon the second step of that small pile,
Surrounded by those wild unpeopled hills,
He sat, and ate his food in solitude: 15
And ever, scattered from his palsied hand,
That, still attempting to prevent the waste,
Was baffled still, the crumbs in little showers
Fell on the ground; and the small mountain birds,
Not venturing yet to peck their destined meal,   20
Approached within the length of half his staff.

Him from my childhood have I known; and then
He was so old, he seems not older now;
He travels on, a solitary Man,
So helpless in appearance, that for him   25
The sauntering Horseman throws not with a slack
And careless hand his alms upon the ground,
But stops,—that he may safely lodge the coin
Within the old Man's hat; nor quits him so,
But still, when he has given his horse the rein,   30

Watches the aged Beggar with a look
Sidelong, and half-reverted. She who tends
The toll-gate, when in summer at her door
She turns her wheel, if on the road she sees
The aged Beggar coming, quits her work,   35
And lifts the latch for him that he may pass.
The post-boy, when his rattling wheels o'ertake
The aged Beggar in the woody lane,
Shouts to him from behind; and, if thus warned
The old Man does not change his course, the boy   40
Turns with less noisy wheels to the roadside,
And passes gently by, without a curse
Upon his lips, or anger at his heart.

He travels on, a solitary Man;
His age has no companion. On the ground   45
His eyes are turned, and, as he moves along,
They move along the ground; and, evermore,
Instead of common and habitual sight
Of fields with rural works, of hill and dale,
And the blue sky, one little span of earth   50
Is all his prospect. Thus, from day to day,
Bow-bent, his eyes for ever on the ground,
He plies his weary journey; seeing still,
And seldom knowing that he sees, some straw,
Some scattered leaf, or marks which, in one track,   55
The nails of cart or chariot-wheel have left
Impressed on the white road,—in the same line,
At distance still the same. Poor Traveller!
His staff trails with him; scarcely do his feet
Disturb the summer dust; he is so still   60
In look and motion, that the cottage curs,
Ere he has passed the door, will turn away,
Weary of barking at him. Boys and girls,
The vacant and the busy, maids and youths,

And urchins newly breeched—all pass him by;　　　　65
Him even the slow-paced waggon leaves behind.

But deem not this Man useless—Statesmen! ye
Who are so restless in your wisdom, ye
Who have a broom still ready in your hands
To rid the world of nuisances; ye proud,　　　　70
Heart-swoln, while in your pride ye contemplate
Your talents, power, or wisdom, deem him not
A burden of the earth! 'Tis Nature's law
That none, the meanest of created things,
Of forms created the most vile and brute,　　　　75
The dullest or most noxious, should exist
Divorced from good—a spirit and pulse of good,
A life and soul, to every mode of being
Inseparably linked. Then be assured
That least of all can aught—that ever owned　　　　80
The heaven-regarding eye and front sublime
Which man is born to—sink, howe'er depressed,
So low as to be scorned without a sin;
Without offence to God cast out of view;
Like the dry remnant of a garden-flower　　　　85
Whose seeds are shed, or as an implement
Worn out and worthless. While from door to door,
This old Man creeps, the villagers in him
Behold a record which together binds
Past deeds and offices of charity,　　　　90
Else unremembered, and so keeps alive
The kindly mood in hearts which lapse of years,
And that half-wisdom half-experience gives,
Make slow to feel, and by sure steps resign
To selfishness and cold oblivious cares.　　　　95
Among the farms and solitary huts,
Hamlets and thinly-scattered villages,
Where'er the aged Beggar takes his rounds,

The mild necessity of use compels
To acts of love; and habit does the work   100
Of reason; yet prepares that after-joy
Which reason cherishes. And thus the soul,
By that sweet taste of pleasure unpursued,
Doth find herself insensibly disposed
To virtue and true goodness. Some there are,   105
By their good works exalted, lofty minds
And meditative, authors of delight
And happiness, which to the end of time
Will live, and spread, and kindle: even such minds
In childhood, from this solitary Being,   110
Or from like wanderer, haply have received
(A thing more precious far than all that books
Or the solicitudes of love can do!)
That first mild touch of sympathy and thought,
In which they found their kindred with a world   115
Where want and sorrow were. The easy man
Who sits at his own door,—and, like the pear
That overhangs his head from the green wall,
Feeds in the sunshine; the robust and young,
The prosperous and unthinking, they who live   120
Sheltered, and flourish in a little grove
Of their own kindred;—all behold in him
A silent monitor, which on their minds
Must needs impress a transitory thought
Of self-congratulation, to the heart   125
Of each recalling his peculiar boons,
His charters and exemptions; and, perchance,
Though he to no one give the fortitude
And circumspection needful to preserve
His present blessings, and to husband up   130
The respite of the season, he, at least,
And 'tis no vulgar service, makes them felt.

Yet further.—Many, I believe, there are
Who live a life of virtuous decency,
Men who can hear the Decalogue and feel   135
No self-reproach; who of the moral law
Established in the land where they abide
Are strict observers; and not negligent
In acts of love to those with whom they dwell,
Their kindred, and the children of their blood.   140
Praise be to such, and to their slumbers peace!
—But of the poor man ask, the abject poor;
Go, and demand of him, if there be here
In this cold abstinence from evil deeds,
And these inevitable charities,   145
Wherewith to satisfy the human soul?
No—man is dear to man; the poorest poor
Long for some moments in a weary life
When they can know and feel that they have been,
Themselves, the fathers and the dealers-out   150
Of some small blessings; have been kind to such
As needed kindness, for this single cause,
That we have all of us one human heart.
—Such pleasure is to one kind Being known,
My neighbour, when with punctual care, each week,   155
Duly as Friday comes, though pressed herself
By her own wants, she from her store of meal
Takes one unsparing handful for the scrip
Of this old Mendicant, and, from her door
Returning with exhilarated heart,   160
Sits by her fire, and builds her hope in heaven.

Then let him pass, a blessing on his head!
And while in that vast solitude to which
The tide of things has borne him, he appears
To breathe and live but for himself alone,   165

Unblamed, uninjured, let him bear about
The good which the benignant law of Heaven
Has hung around him: and, while life is his,
Still let him prompt the unlettered villagers
To tender offices and pensive thoughts.   170
—Then let him pass, a blessing on his head!
And, long as he can wander, let him breathe
The freshness of the valleys; let his blood
Struggle with frosty air and winter snows;
And let the chartered wind that sweeps the heath   175
Beat his grey locks against his withered face.
Reverence the hope whose vital anxiousness
Gives the last human interest to his heart.
May never HOUSE, misnamed of INDUSTRY,
Make him a captive!—for that pent-up din,   180
Those life-consuming sounds that clog the air,
Be his the natural silence of old age!
Let him be free of mountain solitudes;
And have around him, whether heard or not,
The pleasant melody of woodland birds.   185
Few are his pleasures: if his eyes have now
Been doomed so long to settle upon earth
That not without some effort they behold
The countenance of the horizontal sun,
Rising or setting, let the light at least   190
Find a free entrance to their languid orbs.
And let him, *where* and *when* he will, sit down
Beneath the trees, or on a grassy bank
Of highway side, and with the little birds
Share his chance-gathered meal; and, finally,   195
As in the eye of Nature he has lived,
So in the eye of Nature let him die!

William Wordsworth (1770–1850)

Index